ON MY KNEES
AGAIN IN WORSHIP

Going From Pew Sitter to Worshiper

KATHY DEGRAW

PublishAmerica
Baltimore

Hardcover 978-1-4560-4268-4
Softcover 978-1-4560-4269-1
PUBLISHED BY PUBLISHAMERICA, LLLP
www.publishamerica.com
Baltimore

Printed in the United States of America

Dedication

This book is dedicated to:

All the women at my In His Presence gathering who have allowed me the freedom to be me in worship and who have in returned obtained the freedom in worship they so longed for.

To the one person in each congregation who worships freely even if they are the only one.

TABLE OF CONTENTS

Foreword

In Psalm 100:4, the Psalmist writes "Enter into His gates with thanksgiving, And into His courts with praise. Be thankful to Him, and bless His name." What does it mean to come before God with thanksgiving and praise? In Hebrew, the word for thanksgiving is "todah" and means: "Thanks, thanksgiving, adoration, praise." The word is derived from the Hebrew word "yadah" which comes from the root word "yad" or "hand." The Hebrew word for praise, as used here, is "tehillah" and means: a celebration, a lauding of someone praiseworthy; the praise or exaltation of God; praises, songs of admiration. The gates and courts refer to the temple of God, the place of Hebrew worship. When we enter into our places of worship, it should be with hands raised in thanksgiving, with an attitude of celebration. Think of what that should look like for a moment. We celebrate other events with shouting, singing, dancing and jumping. Shouldn't we do the same when we enter into the gates and courts of God?

If you've ever wondered what worship looks like—what it really is supposed to look like, then the pages of this book will enlighten you. Kathy will open your eyes to what complete and sold out worship of our Lord is supposed to be. She will share with you her own struggles, questions and fears as she stepped into total sold out worship of our Lord and King.

As her husband, it wasn't always easy for me to see this transformation take place in her life. Being raised in and pastoring in a denominational church, I did not fully understand what was taking place in my wife's spiritual life. To see her motioning with her hands and arms, to have her kneel in the aisle at church and then to see her lay prostrate was difficult to say the least. I had my own questions and fears. But as both she and I grew in our walk with the Lord, God removed the fears, answered the questions and gave both of us freedom to not only worship differently, but not be concerned with what the other person was doing. If you have struggled or if you have questions, or have fears about worshipping God with no restrictions or reservations, then dive into the pages of Kathy's book. In these pages you will find freedom to truly worship God in Spirit and in truth.

Pastor Ron DeGraw

Preface

I am passionate about worship! I love to worship my God and I love to help other people worship our God. As you read this book it is truly my prayer that you would get to your own comfortable level of worship. I hope this book is an encouragement to pastors; that there are many people sitting in their churches already worshiping in freedom at home and ready to go to the next level in public worship. I would like to thank all the worship leaders for their countless hours of preparation and their ability to lead anointed worship on days they don't feel like it. I pray this book will be a tool you can use to further break your body of believers out in worship. I bless the worship leaders and pray as we equip a generation of believers to worship the Lord in Spirit and truth that in return it will feed and encourage you, as you lead us into the deeper places of worship. I thank you, the reader of this book for allowing God to stretch you, for being curious enough to pick up this book and being open to the Holy Spirit to allow Him to move through you. I know this book will set many people free from the fear of man and what people think about worship.

Before one of my conferences the Lord gave me this word and prayer. I ask you to take them in and allow them to become words that speak life into you. "There are no walls here, no barriers, just freedom to worship. Freedom to be you and freedom to be me. Some people will worship by sitting in their chair, some will raise a hand or two, and those of us who have experienced freedom may kneel, lay prostrate, hoot, holler, sing and dance. There is no pattern here, just true desire and intimacy for worship. It doesn't matter what it looks like, it doesn't matter who is staring at us or who hasn't experienced what we have, all that matters is that for each of us individually we have entered the throne room of God. It is just you and Him, me and Him, no one else matters." He just wants our worship, what it looks like to one of us might not be what it looks like to another, it doesn't matter. If we are more focused on how others are worshiping then we aren't focused on Him. Just stay focused on Him.

God we know no limits, we take off spirits of judgment, criticism and fear. We bind and break off the spirit of fear. We invite you to come in and move within us no matter how it looks or feels or if it is a new experience to us. We break off hindrances, division and legalism. We come together as one body to worship You. Come Lord Jesus, manifest your Spirit Father, and let the Holy Spirit move among us.

May you worship Him in freedom!
Kathy

Testimony

Are you a shy I am just going to sing and stand here or do you just lift your hands and are like yeah go God I love you? Are you a person that likes to close their eyes and do all the other things you do and says "God I love you fill me up but only half way"? Do you bow down on your knees plus close your eyes, sing and lift your hands and want to be a fill me up to the top person? Are you a full out overfill me I don't want to stand person like someone I know?

Now whatever you are you need to step that up and go to the next level. I understand if you're afraid of what other people think around you. What your friends think and your family, I've been there. I know people who have been there. You need to try to push past that and go to the next level without people thinking what you are doing is weird. Yes they may think that but it doesn't matter. The only person that really cares is God. You are worshiping Him and no one else. We are His praisers! Just don't do what everyone else is doing around you. If you want to kneel then kneel, but if other people are standing and it would be weird or make me feel embarrassed so what. It's like I said, don't take others opinions in because it doesn't matter what they think, it's what God thinks.

At my church I am on a worship team for 1st-3rd graders. When we are doing a slow worshipful song a couple of us older people will kneel and then almost everyone else on the worship team will kneel plus the little kids. Now we have been taught to get into worship; to be an example to them, but some of them when they kneel they just sit there with their hands in their lap and mess around. You see all over there are problems with how we should be worshiping. The answer is not how others worship or what others are doing so you don't feel weird or embarrassed. The answer is how God is leading you to worship. I challenge you to go one step or even more. Go one step further to the next level.

Lauren DeGraw—13 yrs old

CHAPTER 1

Heart of Worship

It was in July 2005 when the Lord led us to a full gospel church service. I have always been on the charismatic side. I would lift my hands in praise in small churches of thirty to three hundred, even if I was the only one, but here in this church I saw a new way to worship. I remember, the first time I went to the service, just standing in awe of what was in front of me. A choir bigger than some of the churches my husband had pastored, two praise and worship leaders, a brass ensemble, percussion and three guitar musicians. The people were excited! They were lifting their hands, singing praises to the Lord and worshiping Him in spirit and truth.

I, who also like to sing and worship, could barely participate because I could not believe what I had been missing my entire life. I thought to myself, people really worship like this! You can truly worship like this every week? I could not even put my mind around it that churches like this existed! This is what I have longed for, what I have wanted to be a part of. Then a thought came to my mind "*I had to give all this up.*" We were in transition between churches my husband was pastoring and he was to start pastoring a new set of churches in a week, in a different city and they certainly did not worship like this.

The Lord spoke to my spirit during the service and said, "Kathy, will you go to where I am sending you for a little while if I will give you all of this?" I did not believe it was the Lord speaking to my spirit at the time because I could not believe I could have all of this! That I would have the freedom to worship like this, oh how I longed for it. Three months later, the Lord brought us back to that church where we became members. He gave me exactly what He told me He would. That was the beginning of me pursuing God in worship.

We started attending this church and I saw more of what people experienced during their worship. They were jumping up and down with joy, dancing for Jesus, clapping their hands, lying prostrate on the floor and kneeling down to worship the Creator and giving the glory to God. I said to the Lord "I want that, I want to be able to worship like that, to jump up and down, dance and sing your praise!" Well, you better be serious about what you ask for from God, because He is a God who delivers on His word. He has stretched me so far in my worship and has given me more than I could imagine and it is wonderful! I would not trade it for anything. It has brought me into a whole new realm in my relationship with Him and my spiritual walk with Christ. He has poured out on me because I have poured out my heart on Him. I love to worship Him! We were created for that purpose, to worship Him.

I was not always attracted to this kind of worship. In my life I have had the privilege of attending many different denominational churches. I call this a privilege because my upbringing and experience has educated me with what goes on in other denominations so I can relate to the variety of people who are in different churches. Today in our ministry we minister to several people on a weekly basis in different denominations.

In the church I grew up in there was uniformity to the service. We were instructed to do this at a certain time, and then do that and so on. We didn't have the freedom to worship as we wanted, it was very legalistic. As I started dating a man when I was in my latter teenage years I found myself attending a different denominational church where they were very staunch. I had no problem going there receiving a message on Sunday and walking out. There was no thought at this time that I even wanted something different. You could say I was content and probably a little complacent in my walk with Christ. However, it was in my young adult years the Lord got a hold of me as a different boyfriend invited me to a charismatic church. I felt that tug of the Holy Spirit inside of me. The only thing stopping me from breaking out in praise was that I didn't know what the Holy Spirit tug was. I didn't know it was the Lord. So it took me a couple of weeks to determine it was the Holy Spirit leading me in a new way of worshiping Him by raising my hand. I remember doing it but just a little, kind of afraid someone might actually see me do it. After that first time I continued to do it and have never turned back.

Six months later, I met my spouse and was now attending a denominational church again where I didn't feel I had that freedom to worship with my hands raised. Therefore, back I went to hymn singing and standing silently alone in a congregation where I wanted to bust out in praise. During this time the Lord introduced us to a wonderful community of believers who gather together for what they call a "Walk to Emmaus." Here people would gather from several different denominations and worship, praise and serve together. Here we had freedom to worship! In this community of believers raising hands was welcomed. It was through attending these Emmaus gatherings and hanging out with this community of believers that I started to want even more and started becoming comfortable with being different in my worship. A few years after being among this community of believers, I would then go back to my church on Sundays and raise my hand as led by the Spirit which wasn't that often. I know the stares and glances that probably came my way were there, but I had learned I was here to worship God.

We felt the Lord calling us out of that church and attended another church in the same denomination. At this church they worshiped totally different from the first church. They had a praise and worship team and encouraged the congregation to lift their hands in praise to the Creator, to God Almighty! Don't be quick to label a denomination for how they worship. Churches within that denomination might worship differently. Sometimes it can be a group of believers, a pastor, a worship leader or a particular church that inhibits our worship, not the denomination. I am saying this so you don't judge a denomination based on one churches actions or worship style.

After attending this church the Lord called us back to the church we originally attended for years. This time I went back with a renewed sense of worship. I wasn't concerned with what they thought and started raising my hands more and you know what happened? Those people who were part of the Emmaus community started raising their hands more in church, glory to God! You know where that church is today? With two services one traditional and one contemporary, praise the Lord!

We can be church changers. We can change what happens around us. We are not meant to be church dividers and bring strife and division into the church, but if we are called to be different as the Holy Spirit leads and do something the Lord is calling us to with purity, I believe He will honor that.

I have been where you were or are now, a pew sitter. I sat in that congregation not wanting more, not knowing there was more. Now God has taken me from pew sitter to worshiper and I would never go back. My son, Dillon, said to me the other day "Mom if there was a job as a professional worshiper, it would be so cool, you would be so rich, I know you would love that Mom." He is right, it's all I want to do is worship the Lord because through my worship to Him I have been changed. I am so grateful for all the changes He has done in my life and I am entirely blessed to be able to write this book in hopes of accelerating people to get them to be where God wants them to be. It is not my desire that you become like me, but that you become the person He intends for you to be, and you were created to worship.

The Father deserves this, He wants this from us, and He will bless your obedience to worship Him. Worship is just as important as praying and reading the Bible. Study the worship scriptures throughout the Old and New Testament. Worship is who we are and who He has created us to be. Think about His goodness, His mercy, His grace, His sacrifice, isn't He worthy of so much more than we can possibly give Him in our lifetime?

I remember once leaving a church we were attending, we felt the worship was dead. The people were just going through the motions. We wanted meaning, we wanted feeling, and our spirit inside was just crying out to worship. Worship is the essence of our being. It is what holds us up when we feel like falling down. Praise changes the atmosphere, worship changes the atmosphere, praise and worship changes the atmosphere! The atmosphere it can be changing is our lives, our homes, our workplaces and our churches. The Lord is calling up a new generation of people who will worship Him in spirit and in truth. "But the hour is coming, and now is when the true worshipers will worship the Father in spirit and truth; for the Father in seeking such to worship Him. God is spirit, and those who worship Him must worship in spirit and truth" (John 4:23-24). This was Jesus himself talking in this passage and commanding us to worship in such a way. If Jesus is telling us, then it is our responsibility to listen and act.

Worship requires obedience. If you want to worship the Lord in freedom and truth then ask Him to enhance and expand your worship and be ready to be obedient. Listen for the Holy Spirits prompting while you worship. Don't create things; don't copy someone else, allow the Holy Spirit to lead you. It is the spirit within us that so longs for that worship.

As God leads you to a new place of worship try getting past the discomfort zone by worshiping in your home. If we read the Bible and pray in our homes, why not worship? Close the blinds (or better yet leave them open so your neighbors can see what you are doing and want that joy of the Lord). Light some candles and crank up the praise music. Sing! Shout! Dance! Kneel! Prostrate yourself! Whatever the Lord is calling you to do. If you can get comfortable doing this in your living room you are a step closer to doing it in corporate worship. Invite a friend over and worship with them. Yes, I said worship with them, get crazy for the Lord together! "For where two or three are gathered together in My name, I am there in the midst of them" (Matthew 18:20).

God shows up powerfully in my living room. It is a feeling like none other. When you get done you just want to ask your friend, "Can't you stay a little while longer?" Often, I need to go back to my office and do some more work for the ministry, but seldom that gets accomplished because I just want to soak in His presence, soak in His glory. I put in some soaking or softer praise and worship music and will just lie on the couch and soak in His presence. Soaking is worshiping and God can speak to us powerfully during this time. I will talk about that more in a different chapter.

There are no patterns for worship, just lift your heart and hands and praise the Lord. Listen to the Holy Spirit, He will lead and guide you and if you are ever in the area or we are near you come to one of our conferences and we will help you break through the discomfort zone. God can do for you what He did for me, just open yourself up to Him and say "God have your way with me, I'm not going back just moving forward." Watch what He will move forward in your life through worship.

Modesty Tips for Worshiping

• Do the raise and praise test before leaving the house.
• Raise your hands in the air to see if any belly skin is showing.
• Do the bend over test and make sure when kneeling or leaning over to worship your chest is completely covered.
• Make sure when bending over you don't have bare skin on your back where your pants and shirt meet.
• Any of these situations can easily be fixed by layering your shirts or wearing a long tank underneath!

Amber DeGraw—15 years old

CHAPTER 2

Lifting Hands in Adoration

All through the Bible you see scriptures of people bowing down or lying prostrate yet many of us are afraid to even raise our hands in worship. We feel that gentle tug inside, it is the Holy Spirit within us. We feel like we should do something like raise our hands but then we look to the left and look to the right and see no one else doing it. We see our friends and family nearby and we are concerned about what it looks like and if they are doing it. We want to worship the Lord in a new way but we are scared, we are bound by fear of the unknown.

When you are praying or worshiping in any situation you can lift your hands in praise and adoration to God. When you lift your hands to God in prayer or song you are releasing the Holy Spirit, showing Him you adore Him and you are saying "God I am open to you and a touch of Your presence." You are worshiping and exalting Him for who He is, the King of Kings and Lord of Lords.

"Let us come before His presence with thanksgiving; Let us shout joyfully to Him with psalms" (Psalm 95:2). The word thanksgiving (todah) according to Strongs #8426 is derived from the verb yadah (Strongs H3034). It means to hold out the hand, an extension of the hand, especially to revere or worship with extended hands. It is to thank and praise God with one's hands extended.

Throughout the Bible it shows us scriptures of the strength and power that comes through our fingers, hands and arms. Let's take a look at these scriptures and what they say about us.

Fingers

Our fingers are a symbol of strength and power in our prayer, praise and worship. Look at what God did with His fingers "Then the LORD delivered to me two tablets of stone written with the finger of God, and on them were all the words which the LORD had spoken to you on the mountain from the midst of the fire in the day of the assembly" (Deut. 9:10). God wrote on a stone tablet with His fingers.

"This they said, testing Him, that they might have something of which to accuse Him. But Jesus stooped down and wrote on the ground with His finger, as though He did not hear." Here in John 8:6 Jesus used His finger to convict people of their sin and set a woman free from her sin.

"When I consider Your heavens, the work of Your fingers, the moon and the stars, which You have ordained."—Psalm 8:3

"Bind them on your fingers; Write them on the tablet of your heart."—Proverbs 7:3

When you are raising your hands you are also stretching out your fingers. God gave us commandments through His fingers. What are you releasing into the spiritual atmosphere by raising your hands and extending your fingers?

Hands

Hands are a very important tool in our Christian walk. We fold them or open them up while we pray, we lay hands on others to heal the sick and we extend them for a hand shake or hug as a Christian greeting. Our hands are essential for eating, working, cooking, driving, getting dressed in the morning and going to the bathroom. We need our hands! They are important to us!

God also used His hands "Who has measured the waters in the hollow of His hand, measured heaven with a span and calculated the dust of the earth in a measure? Weighed the mountains in scales and the hills in a balance?" (Is. 40:12).

We know that God used His hands to create. "Blessed be the LORD my Rock, Who trains my hands for war, and my fingers for battle" (Ps. 144:1). Right here God is training our hands for war and our fingers for battle. Raising our hands is warfare worship. What if by raising our hands in praise to the Lord we are binding the enemy and releasing the praise to combat the attacks? Wouldn't it be worth it? Think about those days it is so heavy to worship, that you can barely sing a song. What if by raising your hand you could lift those burdens and heaviness and enter into the presence of God Almighty? Well you can! That is what raising our hands does, it lifts burdens, releases His glory into the atmosphere to combat demonic attacks and helps us enter into His presence.

In Isaiah 19:16 it also shows us the strength of His hand, "In that day Egypt will be like women, and will be afraid and fear because of the waving of the hand of the LORD of hosts, which He waves over it." Right here it is telling us in the Bible the enemy cowers in fear with an upraised hand of the Lord. For myself, with the spiritual warfare in my life that alone is reason enough to raise our hands. The same power that raised Christ from the dead lives in us. So if the enemy cowers in fear beneath the upraised hand of the Lord than he has to cower in fear beneath our upraised hand because Jesus Christ lives in me and He lives in YOU!

Moses hands were used to win a war in Ex. 17:11 "And so it was, when Moses held up his hand, that Israel prevailed; and when he let down his hand, Amalek prevailed. But Moses' hands became heavy; so they took a stone and put it under him, and he sat on it. And Aaron and Hur supported his hands, one on one side, and the other on the other side; and his hands were steady until the going down of the sun." I love this verse. Moses hands were used to combat physical war and spiritual war. If it is all I have to do to win this war we are in is raise my hands I will go around with them constantly lifted towards the heavens!

Arms
As we raise our fingers and hands we are also lifting our arms. God designed everything to work together and even our arms have significance when we raise them in praise to the Lord. Judges 15:14 says "When he came to Lehi, the Philistines came shouting against him. Then the Spirit of the LORD came mightily upon him; and the ropes that were on his arms became like flax that is burned with fire, and his bonds broke loose from his hands." Here the Spirit of the Lord came mightily upon him. In Is 11:2 it states that "the Spirit of the Lord shall rest upon you." I want the Spirit of the Lord to rest upon me. I want people to be able to see Jesus Christ all over me. I want to

extend my arms with a great big smile in praise and adoration. I want to be bursting out of the seems to worship Him!

Jesus took the children up in His arms and blessed them. "And He took them up in His arms, laid His hands on them, and blessed them" (Mark 10:16). We want to be blessed, we want to have that child like faith and we want Him to hold us many times. He will, as we draw closer to Him. We will have these moments through visions which I will talk about in a later chapter.

Clapping

Clapping is applauding and pleasing to God and biblical. There are churches in the world that do not believe in clapping or want clapping in their church. People think it represents an audience of people giving attention to a job well done. It is praising our God for who He is and what He has done. If we can clap, jump, shout and cheer at a football stadium, concert, or performance than we should do it for the Lord above, the Creator of the universe.

Psalm 47:1 tell us to clap, "Oh, clap your hands, all you peoples! Shout to God with the voice of triumph!" Clap! Shout! Get excited! Strong's #8628 defines clap (taqa') as; to clatter, clang, sound, blow, clap or strike. Here it appears when they define clap that heaven is going to be noisy! If you think heaven is going to be boring and somber you are wrong. The angels are singing all day long Holy Holy Holy! That doesn't sound boring or somber, they are doing it in praise and adoration to our Father. Hallelujah!

We continue to have clapping and joy in Isaiah 55:12 "For you shall go out with joy, and be led out with peace; the mountains and the hills shall break forth into singing before you, and all the trees of the field shall clap their hands." The Bible is instructing us here how to worship that we shall go out with joy, raising our hands, that clapping and singing praise to our Lord gives us joy. How can you stay sad or depressed when you are singing, dancing, clapping and exalting the King of Kings and Lord of Lords? It also says we will be led out with peace. I need peace, you need peace, we all need peace. With everything that goes on in our lives we could all use a little more peace. If we can break forth into singing and clapping and have it create joy and peace that is fabulous!

The Bible says, we will have righteousness, peace and joy. Righteousness is being in right standing with God. Having the Holy Spirit within you to convict you of your sin, keep you heading in the direction that God wants you to take and growing in Him. After you have righteousness, peace comes upon you. It is knowing that God is always there even when you don't feel Him. It is knowing that despite your circumstances that you are going to live by faith and not by sight and know that no matter what the outcome you will have peace. It is knowing God is your vindicator, protector, provider and everything else the Word says He is. After you have realized you are righteous, and have the peace of God, you then receive the joy of God! Hallelujah! We could all use a joy impartation. Joy personally came for me when I truly started worshiping the Lord. When I pressed into worship it released joy! Why wouldn't it? Who can truly worship with everything they are and not release joy in the process? As I look over the years of my Christian walk I can tell you when I felt the righteousness release and then the peace come into my being. The joy showed up and was evident to others and myself. Where are you and where do you need to go in this progression? Will worshiping your Lord help you take the next step?

Now I am not suggesting you go home and do all these hand movements and gestures and remember this list. I am encouraging you to step out of your comfort zone and enjoy your worship time with the Lord. Don't be afraid to open your hands and let the Holy Spirit move through them. Let it happen naturally.

I remember the first time the Holy Spirit called me to raise my hands. I was in a charismatic church where everyone was doing it. I kind of felt this tugging inside me like I should but I was afraid. Did I do it? Yes, and I have never turned back. The feeling of love and intimacy with the Lord is indescribable. Even after I left the charismatic church and joined a mainline denominational church I would still raise my hand even if I was the only one doing it. Was it hard, you bet! But I will still do it today even if I am the only one in the church service doing it.

The Lord took me through a progression in my worship. Just like I am taking you through a progression of worship in this book. I was in this charismatic church for only 6 months getting exposed to a new way of worship before I would meet my husband and be planted in a mainline denominational church for 13 years. As we entered this church I knew I still wanted to praise and worship the way I was now comfortable with. It was then that the Lord introduced me to the Emmaus Community where people from all denominations would gather together in worship to their Lord. It was during these times I could continue to lift my hands in praise to God. It made it easier for me to go back to my home church and worship freely, by raising my hand even if I was the only one or one of a select few.

I had to decide whom I was going to serve God or man's opinions. "For do I now persuade men, or God? Or do I seek to please men? For if I still pleased men, I would not be a bondservant of Christ" (Galatians 1:10). Rick Warren in his book *The Purpose Driven Life* says "Your biggest distraction in worship is yourself, your interests and your worries over what others think about you." You have to remove yourself from the fact that you are in a sanctuary, auditorium or wherever else you may be with a group of people and picture yourself in the throne room or up on a mountaintop and it is only you and Jesus.

We are uncomfortable with the unfamiliar or unknown. Unfortunately this holds many churches back from experiencing the manifest presence of God that the Bible talks about. I believe just like I was planted in a church where only a few of us would raise our hands, that there are many believers out there in churches who want to raise their hands. If one or two people in those churches would start being obedient to the Lord and the promptings of the Holy Spirit, then we could see a breakout and breakthrough in our churches. I know there are many people in conservative churches that want to worship this way and that do worship that way, just not in their churches. How do I know? Because they are in my meetings worshiping in freedom and then go back to their churches and quench the Holy Spirit because they are afraid to stand out or be different. They have been trained and equipped through conferences to adore Jesus for who He is and they want the freedom, but many don't know how to get it. They don't know how to be different and are afraid they will cause an uprising by being who they truly want to be and they are being held back from their full potential in Christ.

Don't be afraid to be different, Jesus wasn't. He told us we aren't welcome in our hometown and that we would receive persecution. He died on the cross for us, was whipped, stripped, beaten and died a gruesome death. Doesn't He deserve us stepping out of our comfort zone and stepping into the presence of God? Break your alabaster box! Pour out sweet perfume on Him in your praise and YES in your church! Be a church changer!

In the Bible, many forms of praise are listed throughout the scriptures such as singing and shouting, standing in honor, kneeling, dancing, and making a joyful noise, playing musical instruments and raising hands. Every part of your body should be permeating and spilling out to worship Him. How that may look to one person will differ and vary to how it may look to another person. Let's try to be careful not to judge and just allow the Holy Spirit to move through each one of us on an individual basis.

Rick Warren says it best in his book *The Purpose Driven Life*; "When Jesus said you must "worship in spirit," He wasn't referring to the Holy Spirit, but to your spirit. Made in God's image, you are a spirit that resides in a body, and God designed your spirit to communicate with Him. Worship is your spirit responding to God's spirit." I don't know about you but my spirit man inside me has a party when I respond to God's spirit.

One thing worship costs us is our self-centeredness. You cannot exalt God and yourself at the same time. You don't worship to be seen by others or to please yourself. You deliberately shift the focus off yourself. When Jesus said, "Love God with all your strength" (Deut 6:5). He pointed out that worship takes effort and energy. It is not always convenient or comfortable, and sometimes worship is a sheer act of the will, a willing sacrifice. It is not always a feeling. We don't do it based on our outward actions and feelings. It is a deep desire of the will, knowing that despite our circumstances we were created to worship.

I want to worship our Creator in all splendor and majesty. I want to be available for what He wants to do in my life. Can you set aside your religion, tradition and legalism and allow the Holy Spirit to move through you and the people amidst you? Yes it's hard, it may take a while, but I guarantee you Jesus Christ will meet you there in your worship!

Testimony

Freedom in worship has become a learning process for me in the weeks and months I have participated in Kathy DeGraw's Ministry. As we gather to worship each week, we are encouraged by Kathy to let our hearts be captured by Jesus and express our praises to Him. Some may kneel in humble adoration while others lay prostrate in a spirit of humility. I have stepped out of my comfort zone to dance in worship, and at other times feel led to wave flags in the midst of praise to our King. Learning to praise and honor God this way, releases a spiritual outpouring of adoration that ushers in His presence.

Pam Kamstra

Testimony

There are two streamers and one flag in my basement next to the CD player. They have not always been there; but I have not always worshiped the way I do now. I was introduced to the use of flags and streamers in worship at In His Presence, a gathering at Kathy DeGraw's home. It was there that I felt freedom to start worshiping in a way that brought glory to God, but was not accepted in other venues where Christian's gather. That was several years ago, and now I feel comfortable enough, so that I have two large flags I keep in the prayer room at my church and bring out for our worship and prayer meetings on Wednesday nights.

Tiff

CHAPTER 3

Freedom to Worship

The Lord had brought me a long way in my worship. I was enjoying what He was doing through my worship at our church on Wednesdays and Sundays. I could not wait to get back to worship Him again. I went to church every time the doors were open. He has done so much in my life and I wanted to give thanks and praise to Him through my worship. I went from being someone who just raised their hands in worship, to someone who would allow all the manifestations of the Spirit and the glory of the Lord to come upon them.

Every week during this year of pursuing God and growing in my worship I experienced more and more of Him. My heart cried out consistently for the same thing every week in worship. I would cry out "Lord I want more of You, I want it to be just You and me. I want intimacy in my time with You. I want to focus completely on You." Each week I would cry out to Him, to take me deeper and to give me more. I would tell Him to take away all my flesh so it would be just Him and me in the sanctuary. I wanted to get rid of the consuming thoughts like "What are people thinking of me? What is my husband thinking? What are the church leaders thinking?" I loved the new levels the Lord was taking me to in my worship, but still with all the growth and intimacy I was not totally able to let go of what other people were thinking. There was something holding me back from totally entering in and just having it be Jesus and me. I wanted to be so in tune to the spiritual realm and what was happening in the heavenlies that when I offered up praises to our God I did not see the worship leaders' faces or feel it as I bumped into the pew next to me. I did not want to concern myself with any outside thoughts.

Often we pray, worship or read our Bible and our mind wonders to a different subject or event. I wanted total communion with the Lord. I desired to shut everything else out and had difficulties shutting down my analytical mind. I was constantly struggling with who was around me. I had been told that all the "power" people would sit in front because that is where the glory was and that is where the "power" people worshiped. The comment was not meant in a negative way. The person was hoping to someday be among the few of us who could worship freely. However, some of us, like me, still did not have true freedom and knew people were watching.

One obstacle I faced in my worship was when one of my friends or someone I recently met sat by me or near me during worship. I would be distracted by what I thought they might be thinking about me, the glimpses I would catch out of the corner of my eye of them staring at me or just knowing they were there. I even moved a little forward or backward so we would not catch each other out of the corner of our eyes. As I was trying to press in and press through I would repeatedly cry out to the Lord, "Just You and I Lord, just You and I, that is what this is about". It is not about if people are thinking "Why is Kathy not jumping or dancing or how come the wild worshiper is calm this week?" I just wanted intimacy with Him without the outside distractions of the world and the pressure people put on us to perform.

Worship is not about performance, it is private, and it is intimate. Please do not get me wrong, there were many times it was just the Lord and I, dancing together, smelling the carpet as I lie prostrate in a vision. I have a scrapbook of memories He has given me of those special times in worship. However, I did not want those to be special times, I wanted them to be regular occurrences. I was hungry and I was not going to settle for anything less than spiritual perfection. I wanted deep intimacy to happen in every service where I could spiritually remove myself from the sanctuary and enter into the throne room to worship the King. For those of you who know me, I go after what I want with the Lord. When it comes to Him I am a spiritual hog! I want it all, and nothing less will do!

One day after the Lord had dealt with me on the issue of trust I said, "Okay Lord, what is next? I know we are not going to be like Christ until the day of completion, so what do You want me to work on next?" The answer was simple, true freedom in worship. Freedom from what do people think, the judgments, stares, glances and concerns about manifestations of the Spirit. Freedom that no matter what the Holy Spirit called me to do in worship, that I would be obedient and do it without a second thought.

In my prayer time that day I verbalized the desire of my heart to the Lord. He already knew it, but He likes to hear His children talk to Him. He revealed to me the person who He could use to help me be bold and to help me push through the concerns I was experiencing. My friend was bold and did not care what people thought. She was extreme, and the Lord would use me to tone her down sometimes. I guess He figured she had some extra she could in return impart into me. She had this child like faith that I loved! She was an empty vessel you could pour into! She truly was in love with Jesus and didn't care what people thought. Therefore, He advised me to tell her about the freedom I wanted.

Before I told her, my friend, Melissa and I were in a time of prayer and worship. We gathered together every week and often I brought my list of things I needed answers on or needed someone to stand in agreement with me in prayer. I told her my desire for freedom in worship. I listed about seven things that I would think about when I was in front of people that I needed freedom from and then we entered into a time of prayer.

During this time I was on the floor prostrate listening as the Lord just kept pouring out to me things for her. I keep a notebook during these times so when the Lord is pouring out of me for someone else, I can be accurate and remember what He said. When we were done listening I explained to her everything the Lord told me. She then asked if I wanted to know what the Lord showed her for me. I said, "Oh I didn't expect anything I was just interceding for you." I was thinking this was going to be her day and her time to receive.

However, the Lord gave her a prophetic word for me. He said "Your heart is pure, you exalt Me in everything you do and give the glory to Me. You are not doing this for selfish reasons." He said, "This is about you and Me, no one else but you and

Me." He knew that when I worshiped Him even though I had some outside thoughts that I knew it was about Him and me. Then she explained a vision she had of me. She said, "You were on a mountain top with valleys and hills around; best described by the scenery in the beginning of the movie *The Sound of Music*." She said, "You were on the mountaintop with your arms stretched out wide and you were praising the Lord. He was up on the mountain top too and the grass was so green, the sky was so blue and it was bright. You were just standing on that mountain top praising Him with no one around but Him and you." Wow! Between the prophetic word and vision I knew I was on my way to freedom.

After she left I called another friend, who God wanted me to be held accountable with. I told her my desire and what I wanted her to do. I said to my friend, "I want you to be bold, I want you to get in my face." I said, "If you hear me whining or complaining I want you to get in my face and get bold and tell me who cares what people think." She asked me if I knew what I was asking of her and that the Lord would have to help her keep balance. She said, "Kathy you haven't seen how I can be in people's face, the Lord will have to help me control myself." This all happened on a Friday, later on in the day I told the Lord I want this to be complete in two weeks. I told Him, You have just worked on me with trust for six weeks. I don't want this to take that long You have two weeks Lord.

One of the things that had also been concerning me was "Is my worship style going to affect my husband getting connected with people in leadership at this church?" When I spoke that out to Melissa on Friday morning immediately in my spirit I heard "no it won't," and then later in the day when I told my other friend, she heard "no it won't." I thought, okay what do I do with this information? On Sunday morning before church I had gone for an hour walk with the Lord to pray, praise and worship. During this time the Lord told me that I needed to tell my husband. I have to admit my husband hadn't been too supportive of my worship and we usually didn't talk about the new things I was experiencing. While getting ready in the morning that day I stopped him and said "I have to tell you something good do you have a minute?" I told him I have to tell you something good because most times when someone says "I need to talk to you," it sends your heart racing and wondering what they need to talk to you about and most often fear rises up and you think it is bad. I told him that I was concerned whether my worship would affect his opportunity to get connected with people in leadership at the church and that the Lord told me and a friend of mine "no it won't." I told him I didn't need a response from him and he didn't need to say anything but for some reason the Lord wants me to tell you that and I just need to be obedient. I then left the room without him saying anything which was the answer to my question, that yes it was on his mind too.

On Sunday, I went to church as usual. I didn't expect things to be different and once I started worshiping I felt a freedom that I had never felt before. I was worshiping, dancing, singing, kneeling and truly not caring what anyone thought. The two times I began to think about someone else I would just put myself on top of that mountain with Jesus. I would visualize myself on that mountaintop free. Free from people, free from my husband, free from church leaders, free from everyone and free from myself. I truly felt freedom and it was indescribable! I asked the Lord to take two weeks to resolve this and it took two days. WOW! How awesome is our God!

If we will go boldly to the throne room with our petition, with the desires of our heart, He will be faithful to answer them. The best part is that it carried on into the next week in different areas of ministry I was serving. This affected many different areas and aspects of my life. When I went to the healing rooms on Monday night where I served weekly I had a new found freedom. I usually didn't spend my time in the intercessor's room but this evening I was drawn to it. I wanted to be in His presence. I found myself in an intercessor's room with five other people praying, worshiping and interceding for clients. We put in a CD of glory music and I just laid on my back, arms stretched out wide and said "Lord, I am here to worship You, let me worship You, speak to me, do whatever You want with me." This week there was a new person in the intercessor's room and usually that would have been a distraction, but once again, I put myself on that mountain. Just God and me.

Freedom comes when we relinquish control, when we give up our man made opinions and expectations for what God wants. Freedom comes when we live to please God not man. "For do I now persuade men or God? Or do I seek to please men? For if I still pleased men, I would not be a bondservant of Christ" (Galatians 1:10). Well, praise be to God! I am now a totally dedicated committed bondservant of Christ! We need to be more concerned with pleasing God and being obedient to the Holy Spirit, than what man thinks.

Freedom can come in all forms. I often tell people to start experiencing freedom to worship in your home. When you are all alone with the Lord do something you wouldn't do if someone were watching, dance to Him, raise your hands, kneel or lie prostrate. The comfort of your own home is where your worship can advance to a new level.

I host women in my home every week to pray, praise and worship. In our home, women are encouraged to try something new in the way they worship the Lord or to let loose in an area they have held back or been conservative in. I worship the same way in my living room that I do in church or a conference. By me feeling free to be me it allows the women I worship with freedom to be who God created them to be and how God created them to worship Him. Usually after worshiping in a group of two or three women, it is then easier for them to worship in a small group of 10-20.

We also encourage freedom in our weekly In His Presence gatherings. Women from all denominations and walks of life are invited every week to come for a time of teaching, prayer, praise, worship and healing. We let the Holy Spirit lead our time together. Women will dance, kneel and do things they are afraid to do in front of their own husbands, at their churches or in their homes! Notice these are people from all denominations. Many of these people appear to be pew sitters in their church but give them an environment filled with the Holy Spirit and freedom to worship and they will cut loose like never before! There is freedom, total freedom to worship their Lord.

We continue to stretch people in worship through our conferences and gatherings where we welcome men and women. It gives them a chance to go to a deeper level of worship in a setting where both men and women can let go and let God lead. It is so much easier if someone else initiates it and starts it. Sure, most of the people start out in the pew, but as you move through the day they end up at the altar experiencing the manifest presence of the Lord and entering into freedom. I once saw a woman dancing beautifully before the Lord in one of our gatherings and was deeply touched to see her experience freedom.

Our purpose is to expand people in their worship, to have the fear of what does man think be removed so that they can bring this freedom back to their churches. There are people everywhere in every conservative church just bursting at the seams to bust out in worship. We need to teach, equip and train people that this is how God wants us worshiping. We need to get past the religious spirit, traditional barrier and what people think mentality, so we can give our Lord and Savior Jesus Christ all the worship He deserves all day and night long. We need to get past what the pastor, elders and deacons think and just start worshiping like we were created to. Did you ever think they want to bust out and worship just as bad as you do but are hesitant? If one bad apple can spoil the bushel than one true worshiper can bring out the best! We look at how one person can start an evil uproar, but we never look at how one person can institute change. You could be the one God wants to use to institute change in your church, small group, bible study or denomination. However, if you are bound by fear of man or just stepping out in freedom then how can God use you?

Release it all to Him; cry out to Him and let Him know you long for freedom in worship. And just when you think you have enough freedom, cry out for more. We can always go further in our worship. If we are still thinking about man made religions and traditions, the worship leader has food in his teeth, or looking at the high heeled shoes the person has on in front of us, then we haven't gone deep enough, we haven't experienced true freedom. This is between God and you. Nothing else should be on your mind or consume you more than pouring out your love to Him. Worship Him, adore Him, and experience the freedom you so rightfully deserve!

Testimony

In 2007 I began going to meetings at Kathy's where the focus on God began with worship. I watched Kathy and others around me worship Him in freedom; raising hands, dancing, kneeling and bowing down. God started working on my heart and my religious background to cause me to desire to worship like that and to love on Him with total abandonment. As I submitted and experienced more freedom, He asked me to bring this to the denominational church that I was attending and worshiping in. I became more comfortable with raising my hand and moving to the music.

One Sunday, I could feel Him leading me to kneel. NO ONE in my church did this! But everything in me was telling me I had to do it. I did it, it was hard, but I knew that I was honoring God by what I was doing! You see to me, kneeling before God is one of the more powerful things I can do. By doing this, I am honoring Him and submitting myself to Him. I thank God for exposing me to people like Kathy who has gone before me with courage to honor God by showing freedom in worship.

Carolyn Navis

CHAPTER 4

Kneeling At His Feet

One act of obedience or disobedience through worship can change the outcome of a service. The first few times the Lord called me to bow down and get on my knees I denied it. I could not do it; it was out of my comfort zone. I worried about what people would think of me. I concerned myself with what people were thinking such as, "Oh no the Lord is really moving in her life and dealing with some tough stuff that she has to be on her knees." It never appears to most people that this is our way to worship the Lord or that He is stretching us in worship.

I remember several times the Lord telling me to get on my knees. He would say, "Your being disobedient. How many times do I have to tell you? The song is not over yet you still have time." Finally, I obeyed and stretched out my arms and kneeled before Him and He showed me Himself in such a real and personal way. I felt like in Ezra 9:5 "I fell on my knees and spread out my hands to the Lord my God." The more I started worshiping on my knees the more Jesus started showing me visions and communicating with me during worship. I had to learn to focus on the heavenlies and Christ, not the people around me and what they were thinking. When I did, amazing things began to happen.

The Lord can and will call you to do different things in your worship. While on my knees He could call me to worship Him in song with my entire heart, to pray in my prayer language or to be silent. I stay in tune to where He is leading and let Him do the rest. I don't come with my agenda for worship, only His. I have felt the movement and presence of angels around me in worship. He affirms things to me that were prophesied over me and He uses that time to answer my prayers. He shows me visions for the future and reassures me when I need comforting.

One time, I was worshiping and singing *Pour My Love On You*, it goes "Like oil upon Your feet, like wine for You to drink, like water from My heart, I pour My love on You, if praise is like perfume, I'll lavish mine on You, till every drop is gone, I'll pour my love on You." I had the most incredible experience as I was on my knees pouring out my heart in worship. I had this vision of Jesus standing there in front of me and my praises were pouring anointing oil all over His feet, they were so slippery, so wet and He loved my praises so much. It was so personal, I could see the oil, I could see how wet His feet were. I could feel my hands massaging His feet with oil. They even felt slippery, it was incredible! It was so real when the song ended, I actually looked at my hands to see if there was oil on them.

I am so thankful and grateful for that experience with the Lord. He met me in a personal way during worship. He made Himself real to me and let me lavish my love upon Him.

This was even more incredible than some of my other visions because for those of you who don't know me, I don't like feet! I don't like touching them whether they are mine or someone else's. My husband can massage my feet all he wants and he does, but if he ever thinks I am going to massage his feet, he is wrong! Jesus knew this, so He allowed me to pour my love on Him in a new way, on His feet, and it was wonderful. It hasn't changed how I feel about feet, but I will pour my love on Jesus' feet anytime. Jesus took the vision even further a couple of weeks later as He brought me back to that moment. This time He was massaging my feet with oil! These are the kind of things Jesus wants to do for us in our worship, when we are obedient and pour our heart out to Him.

Another time, I was on my knees and the Lord called me to lie prostrate on the floor and I denied it three times. I really did not want to go to the floor. It is not about what we want, it is about being obedient and allowing God to use us and speak to us in a way He could not otherwise communicate with us. I often found as I was advancing in my worship that when the Lord wanted me to go prostrate He would not all of a sudden call me to lie on the floor. I would start worshiping on my knees and then I would feel that gentle tug in my spirit to lie prostrate.

My friend told me the first time she saw me kneel in worship, "Oh I wish I could do that, I admire you so much." You know what, you can do it, just remove your pride, be obedient and listen to the promptings of the Holy Spirit. Don't think about the circumstances around you, just do it. Start by doing it discretely in your pew if you have to. That's right don't even move out to the aisle. In your row where you are standing, kneel in front of your seat. There you won't be noticed by many people and it will help you transition into this new place of worship with the Lord. As the Lord leads, you move out into the aisle or to the altar.

When the wise men arrived with their gifts for Jesus they fell down and worshiped Him. Here they are worshiping Him even as an infant. "When the men went into the house and saw the child with Mary, His mother, they knelt down and worshiped Him. They took out their gifts of gold, frankincense, and myrrh and gave them to Him" (Matt 2:11). The wise men, a long time ago, knelt before the Lord. They didn't even know all He was going to do for the world at that time. They knelt before Him for who He was. We know everything He has done for us and wants to do for us in the future. Isn't that even more reason to bow down before Him?

How many times has He called you to lift your hands in worship or bow to Him in the aisle and you disobeyed? One act of obedience or disobedience can change the course of your life or someone else's. What if you kneeling down to worship Him led to an altar call and other people coming out of their comfort zones? What if it rose up a new generation of worshipers? What if it set someone free from the bondage they were experiencing? You may never know how your act of worship can affect someone else. Perhaps God is tugging at their heart and they need someone to lead the way, to convict them, to know they are not alone. It is hard to stand out in the crowd. It is hard to get on your knees or lie prostrate when no one else is doing it. The outcome is not our responsibility, only the obedience. Let me say that again "The outcome is not our responsibility, only the obedience." We need to be obedient to what the Holy Spirit is calling us to do. In John 4:23-24 Jesus tells us what He is calling us to do "But the hour is coming and now is when the true worshipers will worship the Father in spirit and truth; for the Father is seeking such to worship Him. God is spirit and those who worship Him must worship in spirit and truth." Do you think there will not be kneeling, bowing down and lying prostrate in heaven? The Bible in the Lords prayer says "on earth as it is in heaven" and all through the Old and New Testament we hear stories and see scriptures of people bowing down and lying prostrate.

"Then the four living creatures said, "Amen!" And the twenty-four elders fell down and worshiped Him who lives forever and ever" (Rev 5:14). We are going to get to worship the Father forever and ever! How wonderful it is, but we don't want to wait until we get to heaven. We can start now!

"Exalt the LORD our God, And worship at His footstool, He is holy" (Ps. 99:5). Do you get this? God is holy, He is holy. We should be exalting Him every chance we get. Too often, we get wrapped up and concerned with what the enemy is doing in our life and we get our focus off worshiping at His footstool. I guarantee you once you start kneeling and pouring your love out on Him you will be so blessed you will want to do it more.

"Oh come, let us worship and bow down; Let us kneel before the LORD our Maker" (Ps. 95:6). He is our Maker, our Creator. Everything we have belongs to Him, He has given us all things. Look at your children, your spouse, your home, it is all from Him. He is worthy of our praise. If we can jump up and down at our son's soccer game then why can't we kneel before our Lord? The good news is we can!

I now look for opportunities to get on my knees. Is the Holy Spirit leading me in a particular song, then down I go. Is there a song that says bow down, then I bow down. I want to worship our Creator in all splendor and majesty. I want to be available for what He wants to do in my life. Are you available? Are you willing to risk pride for the sake of Christ? Are you willing to have your knees get sore and your arms so heavy from stretching them out that they want to drop down to your sides? Jesus wants to meet us in worship, however there are things that complicate our worship and get in the way. Things such as pride, wondering what people are thinking and unclean thoughts and visions just to name a few.

If you have never gone on the floor in worship it is hard. We let our pride get in the way and our own feelings. We consume ourselves with, "Are we thinking this or is God orchestrating this?" We might feel "We are a professional business person and my clients are in the sanctuary or what will my friends think? My suit cost $500; I am not going to kneel on a dirty floor." Ladies are thinking, "Oh no, I wore knee high nylons with my skirt today; what if someone saw I cheated on my pantyhose today?" Or you might be wondering, "Is my shirt covering the back of my pants so my bare back or underwear doesn't show?" People of Christ, who cares! You are on the floor they aren't! They are admiring you and hoping and praying that someday they will be right there with you.

"For the weapons of our warfare are not carnal but mighty in God for pulling down strongholds, casting down arguments and every high thing that exalts itself against the knowledge of God, bringing every thought into captivity to the obedience of Christ" (2 Cor. 10:4-5). The enemy is going to try and distract you in your worship. For some of you he already has. Don't allow distractions and your grocery list to come into your head while worshiping your Savior. Bring every thought captive to Christ. Great things happen when you worship, the devil knows it and is going to try anything he can to interrupt your worship. Don't let him, stand firm and stand strong and raise your voice and hands to heaven and praise the Lord.

I cannot tell you what is in my heart when we kneel to the Father in worship. I love to be on my feet praising, dancing, singing and shouting. But what would happen if an entire congregation began their worship to the Lord on their knees in humility, in adoration. WOW! What would happen if we always worshiped that way? Doesn't the Lord deserve it?

Come Holy Spirit, come and have your way with us, let us bow down and kneel before our Lord.

Scripture

"And the priests could not enter the house of the LORD, because the glory of the LORD had filled the Lord's house. When all the children of Israel saw how the fire came down, and the glory of the LORD on the temple, they bowed their faces to the ground on the pavement, and worshiped and praised the LORD, saying: "For He is good, For His mercy endures forever."—2 Ch. 7:2-3

CHAPTER 5

Worship In His Presence

We hear about people experiencing His manifest presence and often we mistake it for the anointing. People say the anointing is so strong. What they are really talking about is His presence or His glory. It is His presence that is strong, it is His presence that penetrates us and gives us a shot of the glory going through our spirits. The anointing is an empowerment for service. Some people are anointed to preach, teach, heal or prophesy. The presence is His glory, it is feeling the Lord himself. Imagine that feeling, the Lord Himself, touching you and embracing you. We need to feel His manifest presence so we can worship in the glory of the Lord. When we are in His presence we are in the glory, the heavens are opened and we have direct access to the throne. Our worship services should be so full of His glory and presence that we are falling all over the floor, all over the place, because we can't stand up in the presence of the Lord. It is when His glory shows up that the minister moves aside and allows God to minister.

Moses experienced God's glory in Exodus 40:35 "And Moses was not able to enter the tabernacle of meeting, because the cloud rested above it, and the glory of the LORD filled the tabernacle." It was so thick, so weighty and God was there!

Hallelujah! What about the priests? They could not enter the tabernacle, they were fearful to enter the presence of the Lord. But hallelujah Jesus separated the veil for us, the curtain has been torn and now we have direct access to the throne! Christians, why are we not taking advantage of this direct access we have? Why are we not entering the throne room of God every chance we get? God has so much more for us when we engulf ourselves in His love and In His Presence!

I want to worship where the presence of the Lord is. Whether it is at church or at home, I want to be where He is. When I started experiencing a deeper level of worship I noticed sometimes it made a difference where I was sitting and standing. I noticed if I moved to the aisle while praising I could feel His presence more. I will now sit on the end of a row so once worship starts I can worship in the aisle. I can feel the breeze of the angels and I feel the presence of the Lord flowing down the aisle. I have freedom to move, kneel, bow, lay prostrate; whatever the Lord is calling me to do. I have freedom in His presence and I take notice of where His presence is.

I have noticed if I take a couple of steps forward, backward, sideways or go near certain people or the altar, the glory and presence of the Lord intensifies. When I experience this I go near it, I stay in it. Why do I want to worship out of the presence, out of the glory if it is there and strong and real? The answer is simple, I don't. I don't want to worship around people who are interested in coming to church to do their duty, to make their appearance or to see what they can get out of it. I want to be in the midst of a crowd of passionate worshipers who are not afraid to let their underwear show as they bend over in worship to the King. I want to be around people who will weep and let their mascara run as they pour out their love to their Heavenly Father. I want to be where the presence is and that is where you want to be too, in His presence. You want to be with other passionate worshipers, people who get to church and conferences early to get those first few front rows to be as close to the presence, the altar and other passionate worshipers as possible.

After you learn what the scriptures say and that the glory surrounds you, then you will have the breakthrough I did and realize that you a carrier of that glory. Once, when I was worshiping, I took a step back and thought the presence was with the people behind me. I felt the presence stronger as I took that step back. Little did I realize at the time that it was I who had just entered into His presence. He told me the presence is not within them it is within you. You are carrying the presence of the Lord. WOW! Who am I to carry the presence of the Lord with me? But I am someone who is obedient and pure in heart and He follows those who diligently seek after Him and was I seeking. I didn't need to step into a presence, I was carrying the presence!

I recently heard someone say "Worship is corporate, praise is personal." You see, I was searching for corporate worship. Corporate worship is good and while you are growing in Christ, it is good to be around people who are passionate about worship. You become like people you hang around with, so why not hang around with passionate worshipers. "For where two or three are gathered together in My name, I am there in the midst of them" (Matt. 18:20). While you are pursuing worship, it is okay to be around others with the presence you want.

However, don't stay there; don't settle for someone else's "shirttail." Get your own glory, get your own worship. Turn your corporate worship into personal praise. You need to go so deep with the Father in worship that you don't care what the person to the left or right is thinking of you. You don't care if your hair is a mess or your pantyhose have a run in them. You need to put yourself on the mountain top and say, "It's just You and me Lord and I am here to worship You."

The more He gives me the more I want. He will give you His glory and His presence wherever you go. It follows you because Christ is in you. The Lord's presence is always in my home but there are definite times when it is stronger than others. When I walk by my living room and feel a strong presence of the Lord in there, I go into the presence. I am learning that if the Lord's presence is so strong I can feel it, that it is hard to stand in it, that He wants me in it. I have learned if I walk by a room and the presence is there, then I need to be there too. When He calls me into that room, no matter how busy I am or what I am in the middle of, if His presence is there, then He has set this time apart for a divine appointment with me. I am not going to miss it. I may not know the purpose, He does and that is all I need to know. When I am finished with my time in the Lord I might not even know what He did. I might not know what I received or what He downloaded into me and it doesn't matter. All that matters is that I was obedient. We tend to over analyze and think He didn't do anything, but my God is a big God who is willing to give me a continual outpouring. Even if I don't know what He accomplished, I know I have to be there if nothing more than to "Be still and know that I am God" (Ps. 46:10).

When is the last time you put yourself in the presence? Do you know of someone who loves to worship God? Then get to know them and worship with them. Be around people who love to worship in spirit and truth and be around people who love to be in His presence. We need more people who love to be in the presence of the Lord. The presence is for everyone, it appeared to all. "And Moses and Aaron went into the tabernacle of meeting, and came out and blessed the people. Then the glory of the LORD appeared to all the people" (Lev. 9:23). The glory of the Lord appeared to all; not just some, not a few, not many, but ALL. It is for you and for me, for the denominational churches and the charismatic people. The glory and presence of the Lord is for all if we will open up our heart and receive it.

The presence can be so strong. The presence can come across like a sweet aroma, a sweet fragrance or it can be a feeling you feel. I remember a time where I could smell the sweetness. I said to my friend, "Can you smell that?" She said, "No, I only smell anointing oil." We had been burning candles for weeks while we gathered and the candles were inexpensive, old and not fragrant. I knew it was the presence of the Lord. I had never smelled anything so sweet, so enticing, so inviting, so soothing and calming. I just wanted to breathe more and more of Him in.

I remember a time my schedule was clear and I thought to myself, "Oh great I will write my book today." However, the presence of the Lord in my house was so strong He had other things in mind for me. I remember putting in some anointed Christian music and just lying on the couch. I would get up and do a few things and then come back and prostrate myself on the living room floor. I spent my time, thinking, lifting up prayers, taking brief naps and basking in His presence. The presence of the Lord was so strong in the house this day because He wanted me to rest and be refilled after five days of ministering. It was beautiful, I could have cried several times during the day because I was in His presence, so in love with Him. I remember sitting on the couch looking at a picture of the Lord and just crying out to Him how much I love Him. I simply did nothing. I didn't have hard core warfare type prayers, I didn't dance, sing and worship much. I just sat still and enjoyed His presence, His refreshing and it is very refreshing to be with Him.

I remember asking my children, "Do you feel the presence of the Lord, do you feel it?" and they didn't. I was at the dinner table still in the spirit, singing, worshiping and praying. I could not get out of it or get enough of it. I even got frustrated with my family and said to them "I can't believe you can't feel the presence of the Lord that is in this house." I want everyone to feel the Lord the way I do; to experience His manifest presence in a new and profound way. I want people to tell the King of Kings and Lord of Lords, "I love you, I really love you." Often, people can feel the presence when they walk into my house. Perhaps my family could not feel it strong that day because we live in the presence. But this day was different, there was an elevated sense of His presence and I just wanted them to bask in it as badly as I wanted to.

I want people to experience His presence like I do, because in His presence He speaks to us.

In Deut. 5:24 it says "And you said,'Surely the LORD our God has shown us His glory and His greatness, and we have heard His voice from the midst of the fire. We have seen this day that God speaks with man; yet he still lives." God does show us His glory, His presence is among us and around us. Through these times of intimate communion with the Lord He speaks to us. Let's face it, we all want the Lord to speak to us. Why do people go around seeking a prophetic word? Because they want to hear from God. Most of the time God doesn't choose to speak to us audibly, so we look for an audible voice through the prophetic words we receive. However, when we are in His midst, God can give us our own prophetic word directly from Him, dropped into our spirit man. In these moments of God's deep presence, most of the time He still does not talk audibly. But, so often we can hear Him just as clearly in our spirit man because we are totally focused on Him.

God's presence consumes us during these times, it draws us in and makes us want more of these moments with Him. "Now the glory of the LORD rested on Mount Sinai, and the cloud covered it six days. And on the seventh day He called to Moses out of the midst of the cloud. The sight of the glory of the LORD was like a consuming fire on the top of the mountain in the eyes of the children of Israel" (Ex. 24:16-17). God's presence is like a consuming fire! WOW! Have you ever been in those times with the Lord that you actually felt your body was on fire as He was totally consuming you? It is awesome! Be in God's presence so He can consume you!

Testimony

I truly did not understand the meaning of worship, the only thing I knew to do was to raise my hands. God has shown me, through DeGraw Ministries what worship is, and how even my worship time is showing obedience to the Lord. Because of this, I have developed a greater level of intimacy with my Lord that I did not even know I could have.

Tina Russell

CHAPTER 6

Prostrate On My Face

Lying prostrate on the carpet? Who would want to do that? What would cause a person to risk their dignity and lie on the middle of a dirty church floor? They must really be suffering; God must be dealing heavily with them on some issue. What does it take for someone to have courage to go on their face? I'm sure the carpet doesn't smell too good. These are some of the thoughts people around someone lying prostrate may be thinking. The truth is, when you prostrate and humble yourself and put your face to the smelly carpet to seek His face, fellowship happens. It is the place where intimacy meets the Almighty. It is the place where you can directly communicate with God. Where He will talk to you, give you visions, show you your destiny, answer your prayers, and assure you of the salvation of the ones you love and much more. It is a place of intimacy like none other.

I have never ever been sorry that I put my face to the floor and sought Him, the Maker of heaven and earth. I have never regretted the presence of the Holy Spirit coming over me and how He has moved mightily in my spirit during those times. I love getting up from those moments, hardly able to stand or function because I have just been with the Lord. I never regret the fact that people are uncomfortable around me because they don't understand what happens in those moments of intimate fellowship. I don't regret the praise songs that I missed singing, because I was just with the One I should have been singing to. I do not have one time that I was on my face that I don't cherish deeply.

The only times I do regret are the times I was disobedient, and it took the Lord telling me three times to get to the floor. The moments I could have had, the moments I cut short, and the more words of affirmation He would have spoken, if only I would have been obedient sooner. If I would have dropped to the floor the first time He asked me instead of making Him persist. Instead of making Him say "I want to talk to you and tell you something." It is not the only way and time He talks to me, but it is the most intimate fellowship. The way I enjoy communing with Him the most. How I treasure those times. I have memories of those times inside me, those moments are a spiritual scrapbook. Thank you Jesus, thank you Father, thank you Holy Spirit! Come again and visit me soon. I love to be in Your presence.

Worship is defined as "to bow down or lay prostrate." For some of you this may mean to do this spiritually, but for me, God showed me how to do it physically. In the Bible, several times we hear stories and see people falling down on their face:

"I prostrated myself before the Lord; forty days and forty nights I kept prostrating myself."—Duet. 9:25

"Then Job arose, tore his robe, and shaved his head; and he fell to the ground and worshiped."—Job 1:20

"And one of them, when he saw that he was healed, returned, and with a loud voice glorified God, and fell down on his face at His feet, giving Him thanks."—Luke 17:15-16

"All the angels stood around the throne and the elders and the four living creatures, and fell on their faces before the throne and worshiped God."—Rev. 7:11

You too can have this intimate time with the Lord. He desires those moments. The Bible speaks many times about people falling down, lying prostrate and bowing down before the King of Kings and Lord of Lords. How do you get there? How do you start? By seeking the Lord for repentance; for repentance of all the times you didn't diligently seek Him. Pray and begin to ask the Holy Spirit to lead and guide you. Tell Him you're afraid of what people will think if you start doing this. Ask Him to remove your flesh and to help you set aside your agenda for His. Ask Him to give you a deeper fellowship with the Lord.

Begin to expand your worship by starting in your comfort zone. Could you handle bowing down and kneeling in worship or prayer? Starting in this area will bring you to a place of submission. A place where you can get past the fears and the doubts. It can be a place to get past the people pleaser dilemma or what do my friends, spouse or pastor think. It can help you get past your own fears such as; what are people thinking of me, does my shirt cover the back of my pants or is it crunched up and not neat?

Why do we even concern ourselves with these thoughts? We are worshiping our Lord! But we do. Every one of us have had these thoughts running through our minds. Get past it! Worship your Lord, fellowship with Him, He desires intimacy with you. He is offering it to you, take it, receive it and offer Him the intimacy and fellowship back. God will take you to a place and He will commune with you like nothing else you have experienced, if you will just be obedient to Him and the Holy Spirit's prompting.

If you are not able to get rid of what people think one trip to the floor lying prostrate will take care of that. I had been on my knees for a few months when I felt the Lord calling me to lie prostrate on the floor. I can remember it like it was yesterday saying, "Oh no Lord not this, I'm not ready for this." I remember the first time I found myself on the floor. I was in a worship service on my knees and the Holy Spirit was leading me to lie prostrate. I denied it, I remember saying "Oh no Lord not this, I can't do this." Then our worship leader took us in a different direction. He stopped playing the music, had us sit back down and started preaching to us. He then led us back into worship and said "I want you to kneel down, bow down or lie prostrate," anything you feel the Lord calling you to do. I remember sitting in my pew just laughing in unbelief that I was going to have to do this. Laughing at the fact that God was not going to give up on me. He was even using the worship leader to get me to a point of submission and conviction. As soon as the music started I found myself face down on the ground. I remember my husband saying to me afterward, "That was easy for you because other people went to the altar." It wasn't easy. I was one of the first two down on the floor, however I was obedient.

The next time I was on my knees and the Lord told me to go to the floor I denied it three times. I still hadn't learned my lesson from the first time. You could compare me to Peter who denied the Lord three times. I finally obeyed when the Lord told me, "Kathy there is still time left during this song." I remember having my nose in the carpet (even though it was newer carpet it didn't smell all that great). I had my arms stretched out and the Lord was speaking to me. It was exactly the comfort and reassurance I needed and hadn't even asked for. The Lord was talking to me about a prophetic word I had received. He wanted to assure me the prophetic word was truly from Him. He doesn't have to, but He chooses to meet us in a real way when we will surrender to Him and remove our flesh from the situation. When I got up it felt so cleansing. I felt so clean and fresh like I had just been washed with the living water that the Lord offers. I don't know what I was even washed or cleansed of. My best assumption was the negativity, persecution and the spiritual warfare I had been in for the previous two weeks. It doesn't matter what I was cleansed from, it felt simply great and refreshing.

I believe the Lord honored me with that moment because I had been faithful in spite of the negativity being spoken into my life and ministry. I did not offer back any harsh words but simply blew the offenses off. It was challenging living in that period of time, but I did not feed the spiritual war that was going on. I simply stood fast and remained faithful to God my Father, to Jesus my Lord and Savior, and to the promptings of the Holy Spirit. I persevered through the situation and He refreshed me. How awesome! He will do that for you too if you will allow Him to. He comes to be your comforter, your guide, your companion and your friend. He wants to encourage you, lift you up and give you a time of refreshing. If I would not have been obedient, I would not have been refreshed and renewed.

Listen to the Holy Spirit's promptings and don't let pride and fear get in your way. Be obedient to the Lord and don't let what people will think get in your way of being who He is calling you to be for Him and His glory.

When we are on our face to the ground it is about God and us. It is not a time to say "Look at me, look at what I am doing or look at where the Lord is calling me." This is not to be taken as an "arrival moment" in the Lord. We need to come humbly before the throne. One way you can accomplish coming humbly before the throne is to try and draw the least attention to yourself as possible. You can do this by always sitting on the end of a row of seats. That way you can easily take one step over and worship or pray in the aisle. Listen for the Holy Spirit's promptings and how He wants you to worship Him.

As the Holy Spirit leads I usually end up on my knees first. During this time, I worship, sing and commune with Him. If He leads me, then I will lie prostrate on the ground right there. I don't stand up, walk down to the front and lie in front of the altar or stage for everyone to see. I would be obedient and have done this as the Lord leads me to in a conference or arena type event. However, at my church, people don't worship at the altar and during my church service this is a personal and intimate time between God and me. I want to respect my church practices and I can worship my Father in a discreet way in the aisle. If you know the Lord is calling you to walk up front and you have bound your flesh and there is no pride or attention in you then, by all means, listen to the Holy Spirit. However, we don't have to be in front of everyone to have God move in our lives. He will meet us right where we are.

One time, I remember going down on my face during worship and when worship was done, fifteen minutes later, I truly didn't want to get up. I felt like I was having a one on one conversation with God. We were just going back and forth and He was answering so many questions. It was wonderful. I was kind of concerned that the person in front of me worshiping didn't step on me, but I easily forgot about that once I started communing with the Father.

When I lie prostrate, I often balance my head in the air and have my arms spread out wide like Jesus did on the cross. There is something about having your face directly in the carpet, not balanced on your hands and not to the side but directly in the carpet. I encourage you to try different head and arm positions while lying prostrate, to discover for yourself the position that brings you the most intimacy with Christ.

Lying prostrate takes endurance and after a while it can become harder to breath. To be lying flat on your stomach and balancing your head takes strength. You feel like you are in a spiritual marathon. Try to endure, the longer you stay down the more you will receive, but it's not all about receiving. It is about giving yourself to the Lord. When my endurance is starting to weaken, I will turn over and lie on my back. I will spread my arms wide to surrender to the Lord. It is in times like these that I often just pour my love on Him. I tell Him several times "I love you." When is the last time you have said to God, "I Love You"? He knows you love Him. But we as parents and spouses like to hear our loved ones say "I love you" our Heavenly Father also likes to hear us say "I Love You."

In times on my back I may pray in English or if I am getting distracted, I will pray in the spirit to help get my mind focused again. I will worship, think about Him, take myself back to a previous vision, or rest and wait for Him to speak to me. How often do we still ourselves to just listen to God? To say, "God I am here, have your way with me."

I encourage you to lie prostrate, however, we know God ministers to us in different ways. The Associate Director of our ministry and I started out as best friends. When she moved back to the area in which I was living we started having a weekly praise, worship and prayer session with the Lord. We would meet 2 hours 1 day a week and offer ourselves to the Lord in what ever way He wanted to move. One week, as I was praying over Melissa, (I wasn't even touching her) the Lord took her into a trance. In the Bible, people also went into a trance such as in Acts 22:17, "Now it happened, when I returned to Jerusalem and was praying in the temple, that I was in a trance and saw Him saying to me." It was an awesome experience for her and we both said "Next week let's expect the Lord to do it for both of us." We came expecting a move of the Holy Spirit and we received it! However, we both experienced it in different ways. As we both stood with our backs to the couches, the Lord once again took Melissa into a trance. However, with me He called me to lie prostrate. I wanted to go into a trance, I was waiting for it, however if you really want to experience the presence of the Lord you can't create that moment. I know some people fall on purpose. We call them courtesy drops, or some get weak and can't stand any longer but, that is not what I wanted to do. I wanted genuine fellowship and communion with the Lord. So where did I go? To the floor! The times that I have gone into a trance have been good, but so are the times lying prostrate on the floor dialoging and communicating with the Father. I cannot create a trance. I can't get to that point of intimacy by making myself "fall", which I don't believe in doing. However, I can lie prostrate. It's easy, God accepts it and it's my way of saying "Okay Lord whatever you want to do I am willing and able." Let's talk God, let's fellowship, tell me what you want me to do, answer my prayer, show me the answer to my disappointment or why something didn't happen that I believed would happen. Meet me hear Father, minister to your child and your daughter. I am here, I am open to hear You and receive what You have for me. It is also a noted biblical experience. "The utterance of him who hears the words of God, and has the knowledge of the Most High, who sees the vision of the Almighty, who falls down, with eyes wide open" (Num. 24:16). The great thing about lying prostrate is that you can do it, anytime, anywhere, whether in prayer, worship or a service. God will meet you there when the intentions of your heart are pure.

Why did people in the Bible fall at Jesus' feet, lie prostrate or kneel? There are several different biblical reasons I would like to explore with you.

We fall at Jesus' feet for healing. "And behold, one of the rulers of the synagogue came, Jairus by name. And when he saw Him, he fell at His feet" (Mark 5:22). Jesus is the healer and Jairus came to Jesus; he wanted his daughter healed. Jairus a leader, an important man was not concerned with fear of man, he fell at Jesus' feet for healing on behalf of his daughter.

A woman fell at His feet for the deliverance of her daughter. "For a woman whose young daughter had an unclean spirit heard about Him, and she came and fell at His feet" (Mark 7:25). She knew the severity of her daughter's condition and was desperate for freedom for her daughter.

Even the demons came down and fell before Him. "When he saw Jesus, he cried out, fell down before Him" (Luke 8:28). If the demons, the ones who hate Jesus, come and fall at His feet, shouldn't us lovers of Jesus fall at His feet? We should be doing it more!

They fell at His feet for a praise offering! "And one of them, when he saw that he was healed, returned, and with a loud voice glorified God, and fell down on his face at His feet, giving Him thanks" (Luke 17:15-16). The one healed was so grateful, so thankful, He took his attitude of praise and fell at His feet. He fell at His feet and worshiped Him for his healing. How awesome!

Unclean spirits fell down and acknowledged Him. "Unclean spirits, whenever they saw Him, fell down before Him and cried out, saying, "You are the Son of God" (Mark 3:11). The evil spirits had fear of the Lord, we need more fear of the Lord in our lives.

In heaven the living creatures fall down and worship before the throne of God and we prostrate ourselves to worship the Lord God Almighty. "All the angels stood around the throne and the elders and the four living creatures, and fell on their faces before the throne and worshiped God" (Rev. 7:11). We will be doing it in heaven, let's get the party started now! The Lord's prayer says "On earth as it is in heaven," lets start bringing heaven to earth and start prostrating before the Lord in the spiritual realm. What happens in the natural happens in the spiritual, and what happens in the spiritual happens in the natural. Why not start doing in the natural what we will be doing in the spiritual?

Jesus went prostrate to pray to the Father. "He went a little farther and fell on His face and prayed" (Matt 26:39). Jesus himself laid prostrate, and if Jesus the Son of God did it, we should do it. He prostrated Himself during prayer time. He cried out to the Father "Take this cup from me yet not my will but yours be done." His surrender, His prostrating Himself before the Lord led Him to complete obedience with the Father.

When you fall on your face to the Lord, He shows up! "They fell on their faces and the glory of the Lord appeared to them" (Num. 20:6). It is simple, there is something about having your face buried in the carpet that makes the Father appear.

In the Bible they fell on their face for revelation and direction. "When there was no water they fell on their faces and went to the Lord. God, therefore, brought them instruction to bring forth the rod to the rock and it produced water" (Num. 20:2-11).

I encourage you with all you have received about lying prostrate, to try it during your personal prayer time. Do you often fall asleep while praying or does your mind wonder? When you lie prostrate during prayer time you can't always get your position comfortable and that can be a good thing. It keeps you awake, alert and focused on your Heavenly Father. Do it in the privacy of your home at first so you can get comfortable with it. It could also make it easier for you to step into obedience when the Lord calls you to do it publicly. Intimacy with the Almighty is created with obedience. Will you be obedient today?

Scripture

"Do you not fear Me?' says the Lord.' Will you not tremble at My presence, who have placed the sand as the bound of the sea, by a perpetual decree that it cannot pass beyond it? And though its waves toss to and fro, yet they cannot prevail; though they roar, yet they cannot pass over it." (Jeremiah 5:22)

CHAPTER 7

Glory of God

One of my friends donated a book to my ministry called *God's Eye View* by Tommy Tenney. Her intentions were for me to pass it along to someone through our book ministry. Little did she know I would read it before passing it along. (It was part of our used book ministry where we pass on books that have been read and loved by others.) The subtitle "Worshiping Your Way to a Higher Perspective" caught my attention as I had been hungry for more worship and was starting to write my own book on worship.

About the time I finished this book I was getting ready to go on vacation. My friend had given me three other books by this author, so I grabbed two of them to take with me. As I started reading *God Chasers* by Tommy Tenney, I was hooked. God's hand was in this and He knew this was the right time to capture my heart. He put this book in my hands at a particular time when I had been asking Him and crying out to Him to take me deeper with Him. The last year of my life had been a year of accelerated spiritual growth and cleansing. God had stretched me in my worship of Him. He had answered all my pleas to take me deeper, teach me more, peel me and strip me like an onion until there was nothing left of the flesh. I had been asking Him the last couple of weeks during my worship to take me deeper, to not let me care about what people think and how I worship.

What is this great book about you may be asking? Receiving more and more of God, and the more we get we are still not satisfied with. The more of God we get the hungrier we leave our worship services and the more we want of Him, the deeper we want to go. God answered my prayer! He was giving me more and taking me deeper with Him. Hallelujah! Praise the Lord for answered prayer!

I started reading this book on a Saturday, I don't know why, I usually clean the house. This was a Saturday before we were to start a vacation and the packing was pretty much done. I had experienced a couple of long weeks of ministry and had done a lot of deliverance prayer sessions. I was in need of my time to refresh in the Word of God and spend time in the arms of my Lord and Savior. This book was easy reading and immediately captured my attention, a plus for me! I found myself feeling the same way Tommy did. I wanted more out of worship, but not just for myself but for the church, for the body of Christ. Even though I go to a wonderful church, I still want more for our church. I want more for the women I talk to who are bound in fear and don't feel free to worship. Who day in and day out "wish" they could worship like I do, but that are bound in fear of "What will people think"? Oh how my heart's desire is to set people free from fear and of being a people pleaser. What must the Lord think when we hold back our worship to Him, because we are afraid of what the ministry team will think or our friends across the aisle? How He must grieve. He has so many blessings He wants to pour out to us during our worship. If we will only give to Him, we will receive something much greater. Even though it is not our intention to receive something in return.

Most of us grew up and some of us still do try hard to please our parents. We tried to act the proper way at the dinner table, dress appropriately and obey and respect them. We have another parent called our Father in heaven. He is greater than our parents. He is our Creator, Savior and sustainer of life. He deserves more than our earthly parents. What about respecting Him? What about being obedient to Him?

In *The God Chasers,* Tommy talks about how the presence of the Holy Spirit is so thick you could barely breathe. How people will fall down in repentance and sob at the presence of the Lord. He shares how worship leaders could barely play their instruments and one even crumpled in sobs behind the keyboard. Who wouldn't want that? Why can't all our worship services be that way? So full of the Spirit that we can't do anything except bask in His presence. People not wanting to leave the church service, event or building because they didn't want to leave the presence of the Lord. Why don't we leave room for the Holy Spirit to move in our services? We are so full of prayer time, music time, sermons and multiple services, that if the Spirit of God wanted to come in and make a move in that place we would have already put Him in our time box. Don't put God in a box, allow for Him to be in charge.

We should be running to our church every time it is open just to worship Him. Ron and I were at church seven times a week when we were pursuing God. Five of those times were for worship services and teachings. We should want and desire to be in His presence every chance we get. What builds us up more than being with Him? Nothing! Pursue Him, go after Him, and give Him all you have. Don't be satisfied for pew warming worship.

The day after I started reading this book I was enjoying Sunday worship at our church. As the worship leader was leading music this Sunday the anointing was flowing off him. I was worshiping God and asking Him to take me deeper. He answered and every time I opened my eyes to look at the screen, instead of seeing the worship leader, I saw the face of Christ. I thought this was what I needed but I was still hungry, I wasn't satisfied. I cried, "God take me deeper, no this isn't deep enough, I am still thinking about the service about things of the earth, take me deeper." When we started to sing the chorus of *The Old Rugged Cross*, it was just like in Ezra 9:5 "I fell on my knees and spread out my hands to the Lord my God." It was Palm Sunday and Jesus crucified me. I could feel the nails go through my hands and my hands and arms flinched when they did. I could feel the nails go through my feet with the same flinching. I could see myself on the cross being stripped and peeled like an onion and being crucified of the flesh. It reminded me of Galatians 2:20 "I have been crucified with Christ; it is no longer I who live, but Christ lives in me." I could feel the Lord removing more of me, it was incredible.

I just knelt in His presence and received the vision He had for me. As I was still kneeling in His presence the song, *Pour My Love on You*, started to play. I love this song and knew it from the first few notes. My husband knew how the Lord used this song in the past to touch my life. He wanted to lean over when he saw the title come on the screen and say, "Honey, just stay on your knees." It didn't matter, I was experiencing the Lord and there is no way I even wanted to get up. As they started to sing this song, I felt heaviness come on my chest, I could barely breathe. I remember taking in about four deep breaths just trying to breathe. I immediately knew it was the presence and glory of the Lord as my right hand started shaking. I had heard about these things and read about them in the Bible, but had never experienced it. My hand would shake a little and stop and shake a little and stop. The Lord started talking me through it and said "Its okay Kathy it's me, receive." My friend had recently asked me if I had ever experienced shaking and I said "no". She told me it was the glory of the Lord and was wonderful! I had seen some shakers in worship services before and, in fact, I told God don't ever make me do that. I had decided shaking wasn't for me and I put God in a box. Before I started experiencing these things I had recently been reading the Bible and had come across some verses on shaking and quaking.

"But a great quaking fell upon them."—Daniel 10:7

"A shaking of the head among the peoples."—Psalm 44:14

"Fear came upon me, and trembling, which made all my bones shake."—Job 4:14

"They will clothe themselves with trembling; they will sit on the ground, tremble every moment, and be astonished at you."—Ezekiel 26:16

During this time on my knees with the heavy breathing and shaking, I also started trembling. My body was slightly shaking and I was getting very weak. The glory of the Lord was all around and I just couldn't hold up under His presence any longer. I found myself prostrate on the floor in a Sunday morning worship service where this does not usually happen. I couldn't even kneel in His presence; I was amazed. I had heard much about the glory. I had experienced it a little but never like this. I remember lying there soaking in the Lord and then I got on my knees again to pour out praises to God. I sang the chorus of this song with my entire being. *"Like oil upon Your feet, like wine for You to drink, like water from my heart, I pour my love on You. If praise is like perfume, I'll lavish mine on You, till every drop is gone, I'll pour my love on You."* When the song was over I could not even stand, but found myself sitting during the prayer time.

It was incredible and exhausting. I have had some powerful visions and God moments, but after this experience I now feel I have truly seen the Lord. I am forever changed, never to be the same. The Father had taken me deeper and I came out of that experience even hungrier than when I went in. Now I wanted even more of Him.

On the way up to Traverse City where we were to vacation, I continued to read my book. I couldn't put it down and by the end of the day it was finished. My adrenaline gets going when I start reading something that good, experiencing God, or just reliving the experience! My heart is beating fast right now just writing this message, thinking about the glory of God! Hallelujah, how awesome is our God to let us experience His manifest presence! God's timing was absolutely perfect. The chapter I was yet to read in the book was on the anointing versus the glory. Tommy talked about exactly what happened to me; not being able to breath in God's presence. He referred it to the Old Testament when the priests went into the tabernacle to present offerings. "And it came to pass, when the priests came out of the holy place, that the cloud filled the house of the LORD, so that the priests could not continue ministering because of the cloud; for the glory of the LORD filled the house of the LORD" (1 Kings 8:10-11).

During our time in Traverse City the Lord continued to move in my life. After finishing *The God Chasers* I began to read *The God Catchers*. Christian books are wonderfully inspired by the Holy Spirit through authors. I love reading and am extremely grateful to authors for their obedience to the Lord. However, my spirit awakens when what I have read in a Christian book can be found in scripture. I prayed about what to read in the Bible and God took me to Daniel. I was so hungry it was like I was reading Daniel for the first time and couldn't put it down. I know it had been quite a while since I've read Daniel, and this time the book came alive to me. Isn't that great with scripture? Every time we read it we can pick up something new. As I was reading Daniel, I came across chapter 10, and as I read it I discovered I had just lived a similar experience.

"And I, Daniel, alone saw the vision, for the men who were with me did not see the vision; but a great terror fell upon them, so that they fled to hide themselves. Therefore I was left alone when I saw this great vision, and no strength remained in me; for my vigor was turned to frailty in me, and I retained no strength. Yet I heard the sound of his words; and while I heard the sound of his words I was in a deep sleep on my face, with my face to the ground. Suddenly, a hand touched me, which made me tremble

on my knees and on the palms of my hands. And he said to me, "O Daniel, man greatly beloved, understand the words that I speak to you, and stand upright, for I have now been sent to you." While he was speaking this word to me, I stood trembling. Then he said to me, "Do not fear, Daniel, for from the first day that you set your heart to understand, and to humble yourself before your God, your words were heard; and I have come because of your words. But the prince of the kingdom of Persia withstood me twenty-one days; and behold, Michael, one of the chief princes, came to help me, for I had been left alone there with the kings of Persia. Now I have come to make you understand what will happen to your people in the latter days, for the vision refers to many days yet to come." When he had spoken such words to me, I turned my face toward the ground and became speechless. And suddenly, one having the likeness of the sons of men touched my lips; then I opened my mouth and spoke, saying to him who stood before me, "My Lord, because of the vision my sorrows have overwhelmed me, and I have retained no strength. For how can this servant of my Lord talk with you, my Lord? As for me, no strength remains in me now, nor is any breath left in me."—Daniel 10:7-17

Remember my story earlier of my worship experience on Palm Sunday? I am in awe of God when He shows us in scripture what is happening in our lives. Let's take a deeper look at these scriptures and what just happened:

Vs. 7—A great terror/quaking fell upon them.
- I felt the quaking in my body.

Vs. 8 No strength remained in me.
- I too, lost my strength and felt weak.

Vs. 9—My face to the ground.

- I went and laid prostrate.

Vs. 10—A hand touched me which made me tremble and shake on my knees and the palms of my hands.

- I was shaking and my hands were shaking.

Vs. 11—I stood trembling.

- When I got up I was trembling and was weak and had no strength.

Vs. 12—I have come because of your words.

- I had been pleading and crying out to God.

Vs. 15—I turned my face towards the ground and became speechless.

- I tried to sing but could not, I tried to pray but could not, and I became speechless.

Vs. 17—No strength remains in me now, nor is any breath left in me.

- I had no strength and had to sit down and couldn't even pray during prayer time.

After reading this scripture, I was truly amazed at how God continued to unfold this week in my life. How He used worship leaders, a Christian author and the Bible. Do you know how magnificent it was to see what I had experienced right there in the Bible? Wow! What an affirmation! You know the best part about it, you can have it too. Cry out to Him, be passionate for Him, and be desperate for Him. Seek Him with everything you've got. Demand Him to take you deeper and tell Him you are not satisfied, but need more. He will surely honor your request.

He longs to see people go deeper. He loves this kind of intimacy, union and relationship with Him. He desires us to go deeper with Him. He is not going to force you to go anywhere you don't want to go; that is why you need to ask it of Him. Tell Him you are not satisfied with your worship. Tell him you need more of Him, more time to study His word and prayer. Tell Him you are bored with your devotional practices and ask God to make your times with Him exciting and creative. Ask Him to change your morning devotional routine and throw something new in there for you. Ask Him to make it different so you are excited about Him and can't wait to get back to your devotions in the morning.

I was never a morning person. I didn't like getting up in the morning and some mornings I didn't even like to converse. I would lie in bed for half an hour listening to Christian music before even getting up. It wasn't until the Lord called me to start getting up at 4:30a.m. to spend time with Him that I started to enjoy mornings. He restored my sleep and blessed me for my obedience. Now I go to bed anxious and I can't wait for the morning to come, because I know I get to spend time with the Father, with Jesus my Lord and with the Holy Spirit. It is awesome. Occasionally I fall asleep on Him, I beat myself up and say you just robbed God of our time together, but you know what, God honors the obedience. What are you going to do to be obedient to the Lord and press into His glory?

Testimony

When Kathy was here in Colorado last, I went to her meeting. Kathy gave me a beautiful rainbow colored scarf for dancing, that I think possibly was her own, but I'm not sure.

God was beginning a breakthrough in me in spiritual dancing and Kathy spurred it on. I had been hesitant. It is not easy for me to dance, because I don't have a knee cap on my right knee due to being hit by a drunk driver. I'm not a huge extravert, so dancing in front along with others in a sanctuary takes bravery. I'm finding out that once God sweeps me up into Him, I don't know who else is around, and it is only me and God and my body wants to worship Him.

I have been dancing in my living room. The fabric she gave me is quite big so I tried a smaller piece that I bought, and it does not flow like the one Kathy gave me. Her fabric practically floats in the air by itself. I have only used it at home, just learning how to use it.

God is truly breaking me out and I never know when it is going to happen in a service. I was in the spirit at a service covered up with a gold piece of fabric, when I got up and put the fabric in my hands and sat in the front row. Worship was happening and I looked at that gold fabric and I had the urge to dance with it. I sat there for a while holding back, when finally I could not any longer. I jumped up and started worshiping God with that gold piece of fabric, like I had done with Kathy's rainbow fabric alone in my living room. I flew! I laughed! I loved worshiping Him with that fabric. My body wanted to worship Him, so much in such joy.

I had not danced in 19 years since I had been hit by the drunk driver. After 19 years to move again is wonderful!

Deidre

CHAPTER 8

Prophetic Worship

We long for His presence, a touch from the Almighty. We crave to worship Him and He craves to have us worship Him. How we long for Him, to have Him embrace us. We long for reaffirmation that He loves us and that we are pleasing to Him; operating in His perfect will for our lives. I long for His presence. I want to let Him sweep me away. I want to bask in His glory all the day long. I would much rather be in His presence than anywhere else. I long for Him; I don't want to leave that time with Him, the times He gives me of personal intimacy. The moments He gives me of communing and communicating with Him face to face. There are days it is hard to function, work, write or do ministry work because I want to be in His Presence. I want to be with Him and have Him embrace me the way I embrace Him. To know Him, really know Him in a way I've never known Him before. I want to go deeper, further and to the highest mountain top. I want to be so in tune with Him so that no one else can touch me. Where no evil can befall me and even if it attempts to try, it can't touch me because I am with Him. A place where "No weapon formed against me can prosper" (Is. 54:17). In His presence I know His fellowship, His communion and I know in His presence all else will fail in comparison and fade away. How I long to be there right now, and I can be as the Holy Spirit pours through me. It makes my spirit man inside have a little party. To bring back those emotions, those times of intimacy, to bring back that fellowship, so I feel like I am with Him again. I long for this every minute of the day. The more I get the more I want. I am spiritually thirsty and I can never have my thirst quenched. The more I worship Him the more He blesses me, and the more I pour out to Him the more I receive. I long for more I long for so much more. Give me more God, give me more.

Have you truly felt His presence? His manifest presence that makes you so dizzy you can't keep your head up? The presence that makes you drop to the floor without notice? The presence that is so thick it's hard to breath? The presence that makes you feel like you are in love with Him for the first time? The presence that consumes you, it captures you; it makes you do crazy things. It puts a smile on your face and makes you sway back and forth like you are truly dancing with Him. You can't keep your eyes open because you want to focus on Him; on what He is telling you and speaking to you. You want to let Him take over and have His way with you. The presence that tells you, that you are a spirit being living in a fleshly body. That you don't need this body to feel the expressions of the Lord God Almighty. Oh pour out of me Holy Spirit, tell them how I feel. Let them get a glimpse of You and Your manifest presence. Allow them to go deeper to feel You in a new and profound way. Capture them up into the heavenlies. Oh to feel His presence and worship Him; to be with Him how marvelous it is.

It is in His presence that we enter into prophetic worship. It is when we will let go of ourselves and our man made agendas and simply follow Him. Let Him lead us in worshiping Him in spirit, freedom and truth. When we can totally let go is when we enter into the prophetic. Uninhibited worship is what I call it. Our flesh has gone so deep in to worship, that what we want has been removed. God is truly in control if we will yield to His spirit and let Him use our body to move through us.

PROPHETIC WORSHIP COMES IN DIFFERENT STYLES:

Hand Worship

Raising our hands is only one way the Lord can use our hands to worship. For me the Lord has me dance with my hands. I focus on worshiping Him and He will speak to my spirit and tell me to praise Him with my hands. I let the Holy Spirit take over the movements. It is like dancing with a partner, except you are dancing to the Lord. When a lady dances with a man, the man is suppose to lead; most likely the lady doesn't always know what steps are going to come next. That is how it is with your hands. You let the Holy Spirit prophetically move through you and you don't know what your hands will do next. I remember a time the Lord speaking to my spirit and telling me, when your hands do certain movements in dance it means different things. He will sometimes reveal what it means to me. If it is not revealed it doesn't matter, it is simply wonderful and I want to allow Him to move through me.

Prophetic Dance

"Let them praise His name with the dance; Let them sing praises to Him with the timbrel and harp."—Psalm 149:3

There are two types of dancing you can do for the Lord. One type you know the steps and have taken dance classes.

This is not what kind we are talking about here. I want to share with you about prophetic dance. It is getting up and dancing for the Lord whether you have had professional instruction or not. It is dancing to the music and dancing for the Lord. You are not dancing to entertain people, show off, or say look at me and what I can do. You are dancing a new dance to the Lord. The Bible instructs us to sing a new song to the Lord. You are dancing because of who He is and what He has done for you. You are dancing because you want to please Him, worship Him and adore Him. During these prophetic dance times you will be dancing by yourself. I will close my eyes and let the Holy Spirit guide me, my footsteps and my arms and hand gestures. He is in charge. It doesn't look like you are dancing with anyone or the Holy Spirit. You are dancing by yourself to the Father.

I also have had experiences when I am prophetically dancing and Jesus will dance with me. It doesn't look like two people dancing together, but as I am dancing in bodily form we are dancing in the spirit together. I close my eyes and receive the vision of us dancing in the spirit together. I let Him lead and guide. Prophetic dance is not to be forced, if it is an effort it isn't from the Lord. Keep it pure, keep it simple and be ready for what the Lord Jesus Christ calls you to do.

Don't think you can't dance because you don't have experience. Don't think it looks awkward or concern yourself with what people are going to think. I see myself as Jesus does. I see myself as skinny in this long green skirt and a white shirt; dancing with Him on a mountain top; skinny, beautiful and free. You don't have to wait until you lose weight to dance for Him. I used to think, "How can I dance for Him if I am not skinny?" He doesn't care. Are you thinking of Him or how it is going to look to man? Are you here to please man or God? God can make any man or woman look beautiful when dancing in the spirit.

I have people who know me by "the person who dances at church." I never looked at myself as a dancer and I still don't. I look at myself as a worshiper. I just happen to move around when I worship. If people want to call that dancing it's fine, but to me it's intimate, it's personal and it's private. However, to other people its worship, its dance and its beautiful and it ministers to them, so let it. Keep it private and intimate in your mind, but on the outside allow God to use it to minister to others. They want what you have but are afraid to step out and do it.

Prophetic worship is passion, it is passion for God. It is breaking past the barriers of what men think and our comfort zone, and entering into the throne room of God. It is mostly free flowing in the Spirit and allowing the Holy Spirit to flow through you and in you.

Prophetic Music

Prophetic music is often a song that is sung after a well known song has been sung in a worship service. As worship starts and we all join together to sing a song we are familiar with, the spirit of the Lord begins to flow. As the spirit begins to flow and the presence of the Lord increases, the musicians will be led by the Spirit to continue with a prophetic song. A prophetic song can be one we know or a new song. It usually involves singing over and over the chorus, or words and phrases to the ending chords of that song. One prophetic song could last fifteen minutes just cycling through and over the song.

Prophetic Painting

Prophetic painting is an anointing to paint while you are focused on the Lord through worship. While you are worshiping the Lord, the Holy Spirit will come upon you and give you a vision to paint. He might give you an entire vision or a piece of the picture. As you take a step of faith and start painting, He will pour out more of the design. The Holy Spirit will lead and guide you through the painting as you continue to pray, worship, seek and discern His direction. He will guide you to what colors and brushes to use. He will lead your hand in a certain direction and guide you when to add water or mix colors. He will personally lead you through the entire design of the drawing, and even tell you when to finish and what the name and purpose of the painting is. It is awesome to be able to prophetically paint.

I remember as a teenager in middle school, I used to dislike art class. I didn't enjoy going to art class! I didn't want to draw or paint and I had absolutely no creativity. As we started doing conferences, my friend Michele, who is a prophetic artist, would paint. She started doing these fabulous drawings as led by the Holy Spirit. Seeing her do these paintings planted a desire in me to paint. One day I told the Lord I want to be able to prophetically paint and soon after I found myself doing it.

Prophetic Singing

Prophetic singing is when the Holy Spirit comes on you so strong that you start singing out in English a song that has never been sung before. You can do this in your personal time with the Lord, and there are people who do it as musicians or at a conference. As you open your mouth and sing out the first few words, the Holy Spirit will come upon you and have you singing a new song to Him and anyone else present. It can be prophetic words or insight, or a song of praise and adoration to the Lord. It is fresh and unique and extremely creative because it is a download from the Spirit of the Lord. I witnessed this at a conference I attended and when the man was done singing he fell right there in the spirit. There was such a strong powerful anointing, you could tell the Lord was pouring out through him to minister to the body of Christ.

Singing in the Spirit

Singing in the spirit is in the Bible and is for all believers who will open themselves up to the spirit and allow God to flow through them. As you pray in the spirit or tongues it can change over to singing, or you can start singing in the spirit. This can happen when you are in worship and you don't know the song being sung at the church. The spirit of the Lord rises up from within you and all of a sudden you are singing in the spirit. I like to sing in the spirit when I don't know a song. It is challenging to sing a new song, and if you don't know the song and can sing in the spirit, it will keep you connected to the worship service.

You could also sing in the spirit on a song you know, during the song or as the instrumental parts take over. You might notice if you sing in the spirit a lot that you get the same words or syllables for the same song. When the song comes on again the Spirit of the Lord will come upon you and you will start singing out familiar words. It is wonderful! It can be a tongue of praise, prayer or warfare. Pay attention and notice how your tongue and singing in the spirit will change and you will be able to discern if it is praise or warfare!

Prophetic Tools

The Lord anoints tools for us to use during worship. Tools can consist of flags, banners, steamers, materials, shofars and tambourines. We use all these tools as the Lord directs us.

- Shofar—The shofar or ram's horn is biblical and was blown in the Bible for victory and warfare. We might be led to blow one at the beginning of the service while we are singing and the musicians are playing in high praise.
- Flags and Streamers—Are used to wave and dance with as the Spirit leads. Flags can be all different sizes and are on a pole. They can be plain, one solid color, multi colored, silk screened, and elaborately designed. There are personal flags about 14-16", standard size 2-3' and large flags for sanctuary and conference use. Flag waving is very anointed and beautiful to watch. We love using them and the Spirit will lead us to which one He wants us to use at that time. He will guide us as to the flag color, style and even how to wave or dance with it. Streamers are used in the same way and are strips of different size ribbons and colors attached to a 12-16" stick where the ribbon can freely rotate. You can order flags on our website at www.degrawministries.org.
- Banners—Banners are usually a very long piece of material. The banners we use are a 3 yard piece of material. It is amazing how God directs us to the exact piece of fabric. I have also been in visions where the Lord showed me what to purchase, and have also had a person send me material. God used anointed materials

in the tabernacle and He can still use them today. I have danced with banners, and people I have taught how to do this have obtained freedom in their worship through dancing with banners.

We want to feel His manifest presence so we can worship in the glory of the Lord. When we are in His presence we are in the glory. The heavens are opened and we have direct access to the throne. Our worship services should be so full of His glory and presence that we are falling all over the floor, all over the place, because we can't stand up in the presence of the Lord. Follow the Lords leading, let yourself go, and worship Him and feel yourself float through the air and enter into His presence!

Quote

It is when we don't feel like worshiping that we need to worship!

It is when we don't feel like getting off the couch and praising the Lord that we need to stand and sing praises to Him!

It is when we don't feel the presence of the Lord that we need to press in harder.

It is when we breakthrough we will find the Lord we are seeking.

Kathy DeGraw

CHAPTER 9

Breakthrough the Heaviness

Worshiping through the spirit of heaviness to get to the manifest presence of His heaviness

Put on the garment of praise for the spirit of heaviness! "To give them beauty for ashes, the oil of joy for mourning, the garment of praise for the spirit of heaviness; that they may be called trees of righteousness, the planting of the Lord, that He may be glorified" (Is. 61:3). We often hear people quote this when they see someone is discouraged, which is what heaviness can be compared to. Some might adapt the verse to say "Put on the garment of praise for the spirit of heaviness!" The Spirit of praise is something you have to "put on." Jesus Christ put our sins on Himself for us, so shouldn't we put on praise for Him?

There are biblical accounts of people pushing through the spirit of heaviness in different situations. These can be an example to us as to how we should also push through and persevere through the spirit of heaviness and discouragement.

Elijah had to push through the spirit of heaviness when Jezebel was after him. Elijah was so distraught in 1 Kings

19 he had angelic assistance dispatched to him, he needed nourishment for his body and physical rest. Let's take a look at what happened to Elijah.

"And Ahab told Jezebel all that Elijah had done also how he had executed all the prophets with the sword. Then Jezebel sent a messenger to Elijah, saying, "So let the gods do to me, and more also, if I do not make your life as the life of one of them by tomorrow about this time." And when he saw that, he arose and ran for his life, and went to Beersheba, which belongs to Judah, and left his servant there. But he himself went a day's journey into the wilderness, and came and sat down under a broom tree. And he prayed that he might die, and said, "It is enough! Now, LORD, take my life, for I am no better than my fathers!" Then, as he lay and slept under a broom tree, suddenly an angel touched him, and said to him, "Arise and eat." Then he looked, and there by his head was a cake baked on coals, and a jar of water. So he ate and drank, and lay down again. And the angel of the LORD came back the second time, and touched him, and said, "Arise and eat, because the journey is too great for you." So he arose, and ate and drank; and he went in the strength of that food forty days and forty nights as far as Horeb, the mountain of God. And there he went into a cave, and spent the night in that place; and behold, the word of the LORD came to him, and He said to him, "What are you doing here, Elijah?" So he said, "I have been very zealous for the LORD God of hosts; for the children of Israel have forsaken Your covenant, torn down Your altars, and killed Your prophets with the sword. I alone am left; and they seek to take my life." Then He said, "Go out, and stand on the mountain before the LORD." And behold, the LORD passed by, and a great and strong wind tore into the mountains and broke the rocks in pieces before the LORD, but the LORD was not in the wind;

and after the wind an earthquake, but the LORD was not in the earthquake; and after the earthquake a fire, but the LORD was not in the fire; and after the fire a still small voice. So it was, when Elijah heard it, that he wrapped his face in his mantle and went out and stood in the entrance of the cave. Suddenly a voice came to him, and said, "What are you doing here, Elijah?" And he said, "I have been very zealous for the LORD God of hosts; because the children of Israel have forsaken Your covenant, torn down Your altars, and killed Your prophets with the sword. I alone am left; and they seek to take my life." Then the LORD said to him: "Go, return on your way to the Wilderness of Damascus; and when you arrive, anoint Hazael as king over Syria. Also you shall anoint Jesus the son of Nimshi as king over Israel. And Elisha the son of Shaphat of Abel Meholah you shall anoint as prophet in your place. It shall be that whoever escapes the sword of Hazael, Jehu will kill; and whoever escapes the sword of Jehu, Elisha will kill. Yet I have reserved seven thousand in Israel, all whose knees have not bowed to Baal, and every mouth that has not kissed him." So he departed from there, and found Elisha the son of Shaphat, who was plowing with twelve yoke of oxen before him, and he was with the twelfth. Then Elijah passed by him and threw his mantle on him. And he left the oxen and ran after Elijah, and said, "Please let me kiss my father and my mother, and then I will follow you." And he said to him, "Go back again, for what have I done to you?" So Elisha turned back from him, and took a yoke of oxen and slaughtered them and boiled their flesh, using the oxen's equipment, and gave it to the people, and they ate. Then he arose and followed Elijah, and became his servant."—1 Kings 19:1-21

In verse 4 Elijah needed rest and wanted to give up, the heaviness was so great he asked to die. To push through his heaviness, God allowed him to verbalize his frustrations. God further recommissioned him and a renewal of purpose was given to Elijah in verses 15-17 and God gave him a friend for companionship in verse 19.

Moses had to persevere when he delivered the people from Egypt. Read Exodus Chapters 4-16 for the full story of all he was up against. He had to go through a lot for the people. Moses had to have experienced severe heaviness every time he went to Pharaoh and he denied to release the people. Then Moses, at the hand of God, released plague after plague that affected the people. There too had to be a great heaviness on Moses. As more plagues took affect and more rejection from Pharaoh was delivered, I am sure the heaviness grew even more. But in the end they were delivered out of Egypt. What a party that must have been!

Paul was persecuted several times in the Bible and pushed through.

"From the Jews five times I received forty stripes minus one. Three times I was beaten with rods; once I was stoned; three times I was shipwrecked; a night and a day I have been in the deep; in journeys often, in perils of waters, in perils of robbers, in perils of my own countrymen, in perils of the Gentiles, in perils in the city, in perils in the wilderness, in perils in the sea, in perils among false brethren; in weariness and toil, in sleeplessness often, in hunger and thirst, in fasting often, in cold and nakedness."—2 Cor. 11:24-27

Paul didn't give up; Paul was committed to Jesus and continued the course. Heaviness probably came upon Him, but he looked at the final goal of sharing Jesus Christ and it sustained Him.

What about Job; he lost everything. Satan was allowed to take his health, his family, his wealth, his livestock and his property. Look what happened to him when he pressed through the heaviness; how great his reward was! The Lord restored him with twice the amount of what he had before, glory to God!

What about the friends that lowered their buddy through the roof? They didn't give up and go home. They pressed through, took off the roof and got their friend healed and set free! *"Immediately many gathered together, so that there was no longer room to receive them, not even near the door. And He preached the word to them. Then they came to Him, bringing a paralytic who was carried by four men. And when they could not come near Him because of the crowd, they uncovered the roof where He was. So when they had broken through, they let down the bed on which the paralytic was lying"* (Mark 2:2-4). These men had crazy faith! They weren't even going to allow the heaviness to take a foot hold in their life. They took their faith and put it together with action and it produced healing and deliverance. We need that crazy kind of faith like these men! We need to take immediate action in our lives, to not even give the enemy a foothold to set in heaviness! His friends saw there was no room left in the home, but they wanted to get their friend near Jesus to be healed. So they pressed through, took the roof off the house, and lowered their friend down.

I remember a time during worship I felt heaviness; I felt a weight upon my back. We were in a church service, and about half way through the second song, my friends and I felt it. We started trying to push through by praising the Lord, worshiping, interceding and praying in the spirit. We discovered it was spiritual warfare because our pastor was doing a healing and deliverance service that evening. The enemy was trying to give us a spirit of heaviness so that we would not pray and intercede during the service, (the very reason we came). We did not give in; instead we pushed through and kept praising and worshiping our Lord, however the heaviness did not lift. I continued to feel it during the sermon and afterward while our pastor was praying for people to be healed and delivered, but we just kept praising.

Praise and worship is not always about a feeling. It is about what needs to be done and what we were created to do, and we were created to worship. When the spirit of heaviness comes on us, we need to stand before the throne of God and worship. Putting on praise is like putting on armor; it is heavy, but we have to wear it. We have to dress ourselves in praise like a soldier dresses for battle. You have to push in and persevere just like the men in battle and biblical accounts in the Old Testament.

Webster's defines perseverance as "to continue in a course of action despite difficulty." It is steady persistence in adhering to a course of action, a belief, or a purpose; steadfastness." We had to persevere through the spirit of heaviness and you will too. The Bible says to run the race to receive the prize. We too have to run the race of worshiping our Creator for who He is and who He has called us to be. "Do you not know that those who run in a race all run, but one receives the prize? Run in such a way that you may obtain it. And everyone who competes for the prize is temperate in all things. Now they do it to obtain a perishable crown, but we for an imperishable crown" (1 Cor. 9:24-25).

Worship through the opposition; don't let the enemy win. So often people give in, stop singing and just succumb to the atmosphere around us in a worship service. The Bible doesn't tell us to do that, it tells us to run the race as one to receive the prize. Run the race to worship your Lord to breakthrough heaviness. If we give in, the enemy wins and our breakthrough doesn't come. We then feel like we have left church and the enemy stole our time, because we were focused on the opposition and heaviness instead of worshiping our Lord.

I remember a time our team had to run that race. We had just completed a long day of deliverance ministry and spiritual warfare. This day felt like a roller coaster with the spiritual highs and lows. In the morning, while in my house with a group of women, once again the spirit of heaviness arrived as a couple of people entered my home. We felt it and immediately our intercessors went into battle; clothing themselves with the garment of prayer and praise. One intercessor in the spirit visually saw the city of Jerusalem over our house; after about half an hour of battle the heaviness lifted. It was wonderful, the women in our house were praising the Lord by kneeling, lying prostrate, lifting their hands, hearts and voices! I didn't want to make them leave that day because they had pushed through the spirit of heaviness and entered into the heavy manifest presence of the Lord.

The heaviness I have been talking about is the heaviness that comes upon us in opposition. This heaviness is a distraction, it is ungodly and wants to weigh us down and distract us from our purpose of worshiping God. Heaviness comes in all forms, it can be a presence in the room, a person who enters the room who is weighed down. It can be an evil spirit trying to penetrate the atmosphere, or it can be something whose purpose is to detour you from the task at hand. This kind of heaviness is a weight, distraction or stressor that inhibits the move of God.

There is another type of heaviness that comes upon us that we welcome, and that is the heaviness of God's manifest presence. It is when the spirit of the Lord Himself shows up in your presence. It is referred to as when Moses couldn't stand in His presence and neither can we. When we cultivate the atmosphere by singing our praise, by giving our hearts to Him, by extending all we are, our inner most being to Him; He will enter into our presence and commune with us. He will take us over and envelop us in His flame of fire. He will hold us close, embrace us, wrap His arms around us, give us visions, increase our discernment, equip us for ministry and simply be with us.

It is His manifest presence, the heavy weight of the glory, that we should be seeking and calling forth down from heaven. In His presence, in this weight of glory, you have direct access to the throne of God. It is like God Himself just showed up in the room. Sometimes you feel drunk; you get dizzy, are staggering around and can't function. Other times the weight is so strong so thick with His presence, it feels like your body turns to mush, your legs get weak and they just want to cave out from underneath you. You try everything you can to stand or walk, and sometimes just sitting up in a chair or leaning against something takes everything out of you. You come to the point that you cannot physically support your body any more, and you soon fine yourself on the floor, because the weight of His presence is so thick. It feels like this invisible mattress is laying on top of you just holding you down, pinning you to the floor. You try to get up but no matter how hard you try you just can't. You are limp; you are at such a state of peace you can't even describe it to those who have never experienced it. All you can do is try to invite others to join in and seek Him like you do.

How I long for people to experience the manifest presence of the Lord. It is throughout the Bible, but so often fear rises up and people prevent themselves from entering into that deep presence of the Lord. They don't understand it, haven't experienced it, and are afraid of what others might think. Some people are completely satisfied with where they are with the Lord and aren't seeking more. Others say it's not for me, I am not good enough to experience that, or they don't understand it and shut God off from what He wants to do, from what He can give them. People perish for lack of knowledge; well here people lack the presence of the living God, because they don't know how He wants to visit them. He wants to give you visions of your future, answer your dreams, show you your destinies and give you gifts greater than you can imagine. He wants you to cry out to Him in sorrow and repentance and He wants to wipe every tear away. He wants to just bask with you as much as you want to bask with Him. Won't you bask with Him? Won't you cultivate the atmosphere in your home, in your prayer groups, in your worship services to let the heavy weight of His glory come in? The King of Glory wants to come into your life, your meeting and your church service. Let Him come in, desire Him to come in, repent for what you did not know or want to experience, and let the King of Glory come in.

We don't worship to get something out of it, it is not for us. However, we will end up blessed when we push through. We will have the pleasure of knowing we worshiped with pure intentions and took back territory from the enemy. We could even get a garment of praise, a vision, a word from the Lord, a personal intimate moment with Him or peace from experiencing His presence. He blesses us for our obedience and He blesses us for our worship. He doesn't have to but He chooses to.

That same day, later in the evening as we approached the altar to worship during our midweek service, our team felt heaviness again. This time we were discerning whether it was in the church, upon us from a long day, or leftover from the Sunday service. It didn't matter where it came from all we knew was that we needed to break through it.

I like to move when I worship. I always pick an end seat so I can get in the aisle and dance, shout, jump, kneel, lie prostrate, whatever the Holy Spirit is calling me to do. On this particular day I was doing all I could to just stand up. It took all I had in me to sing and raise my hands. The spirit of ungodly heaviness was so strong I just wanted to lie on the floor the entire time because physically I couldn't hold up. The Lord was not telling me to lie prostrate, so I just stood up, and it was all I could do to spread my arms out wide and say "Lord I have come to worship You, it's about You and me. I don't have it in me right now so I am just standing with arms wide open in surrender to You; in obedience for what I was created for."

I was thinking, people around me must think what is wrong with me. She is usually jumping and praising all over the place.

All she is doing is standing there; she must have had a tough rough day. I was trying to push through with everything that was in me. The next song, I went to my knees and continued to worship in the only way I truly know how, "on my knees." My favorite place to be and the only place to be when words and songs won't do. So that is where I went, on my knees. I wanted a partial worship instead of no worship at all. I didn't come to church that evening to be a complacent pew warmer and let this spirit of heaviness have its way. I wanted to give glory to the King for the marvelous things He had done that day. The healings, the deliverances, the changed lives and the freedom! I started thanking Him for all He had done; giving Him glory for all He is.

We don't always need to sing to worship God; worship comes in many different forms. I love Him and I want to give Him the glory and honor He is due. By the fourth song of the evening, most of the heaviness had lifted and I saw a smile on our worship leaders face once again as I started dancing, singing and praising as close to usual as I could get. I'm sure the worship leader was thankful that evening that He could be used to help us breakthrough. When we enjoy the worship and praise, it encourages our worship leaders. I have many people come up to me from the choir and worship leaders, to say how they love to see me worshiping Jesus. It encourages them and lets them know they are touching lives.

Esther also had to press through heaviness when her people were in trouble.

"So Esther's maids and eunuchs came and told her, and the queen was deeply distressed. Then she sent garments to clothe Mordecai and take his sackcloth away from him, but he would

not accept them. Then Esther called Hathach, one of the king's eunuchs whom he had appointed to attend her, and she gave him a command concerning Mordecai, to learn what and why this was. So Hathach went out to Mordecai in the city square that was in front of the king's gate. And Mordecai told him all that had happened to him, and the sum of money that Haman had promised to pay into the king's treasuries to destroy the Jews. He also gave him a copy of the written decree for their destruction, which was given at Shushan, that he might show it to Esther and explain it to her, and that he might command her to go in to the king to make supplication to him and plead before him for her people. So Hathach returned and told Esther the words of Mordecai. Then Esther spoke to Hathach, and gave him a command for Mordecai: "All the king's servants and the people of the king's provinces know that any man or woman who goes into the inner court to the king, who has not been called, he has but one law: put all to death, except the one to whom the king holds out the golden scepter, that he may live. Yet I myself have not been called to go in to the king these thirty days." So they told Mordecai Esther's words. And Mordecai told them to answer Esther: "Do not think in your heart that you will escape in the king's palace any more than all the other Jews. For if you remain completely silent at this time, relief and deliverance will arise for the Jews from another place, but you and your father's house will perish. Yet who knows whether you have come to the kingdom for such a time as this?" Then Esther told them to reply to Mordecai: "Go, gather all the Jews who are present in Shushan, and fast for me; neither eat nor drink for three days, night or day. My maids and I will fast likewise. And so I will go to the king, which is against the law; and if I perish, I perish!" So Mordecai went his way and did according to all that Esther commanded him."—Esther 4:4-17

Esther was distressed; she was burdened and heavy for her people and for herself. She was afraid for her people and herself that they would perish. What did she do; she prayed and fasted. She pressed in and persevered through the spirit of heaviness; and look what happened in the end; her people were saved.

Mary and Martha were also experiencing heaviness when Lazarus had died.

"Now Jesus had not yet come into the town, but was in the place where Mary had met Him. Then the Jews who were with her in the house, and comforting her, when they saw that Mary rose up quickly and went out, followed her, saying, "She is going to the tomb to weep there." Then, when Mary came where Jesus was, and saw Him, she fell down at His feet, saying to Him, "Lord, if you had been here, my brother would not have died." Therefore, when Jesus saw her weeping, and the Jews who came with her weeping, He groaned in the spirit and was troubled. And He said, "Where have you laid him?" They said to Him, "Lord, come and see." Jesus wept. Then the Jews said, "See how He loved him!" And some of them said, "Could not this Man, who opened the eyes of the blind, also have kept this man from dying?" Then Jesus, again groaning in Himself, came to the tomb. It was a cave, and a stone lay against it. Jesus said, "Take away the stone." Martha, the sister of him who was dead, said to Him, "Lord, by this time there is a stench, for he has been dead four days." Jesus said to her, "Did I not say to you that if you would believe you would see the glory of God?" Then they took away the stone from the place where the dead man was lying. And Jesus lifted up His eyes and said, "Father, I thank you that you have heard Me. And I know that you always hear me, but because of

the people who are standing by I said this, that they may believe that you sent me." Now when He had said these things, He cried with a loud voice, "Lazarus, come forth!" And he who had died came out bound hand and foot with grave clothes, and his face was wrapped with a cloth. Jesus said to them, "Loose him, and let him go." Then many of the Jews who had come to Mary, and had seen the things Jesus did, believed in Him."—John 11:30-44

Mary and Martha had to push through the spirit of heaviness. Jesus said "Did I not say to you that if you would believe you would see the glory of God?" (John 11:40). They had to believe they had to push through, and when they did their brother Lazarus arose and God was glorified.

Mary the mother of Jesus had to press through the spirit of heaviness as she watched her son and Lord being crucified. *"Now there stood by the cross of Jesus His mother, and His mother's sister, Mary the wife of Clopas, and Mary Magdalene. When Jesus therefore saw His mother, and the disciple whom He loved standing by, He said to His mother, "Woman, behold your son!" (John 19:25-26).* Mary stood there as she watched Jesus being whipped, stripped and beaten. She stood and watched as blood dripped from His face, as He was dying a criminal's death hanging from a cross. She definitely is a testimony of pressing through the heaviness.

As I write this, I am once again overcome with heaviness as the enemy continues to attack the surroundings around me. What am I doing? I am taking control and authority over the enemy the best way I know how, by worshiping my Lord, by soaking in His presence, and by making the enemy really mad by using this experience to write another chapter of my book on worship. In Rev. 12:11 it states "And they overcame him by the blood of the Lamb and by the word of their testimony."

Spiritual warfare is real. Before, during and after it can put on a spirit of heaviness. At times like these, when we feel the weight, sometimes it is all we can do to stand up with arms open wide and put on the garment of praise. Praise changes the atmosphere, worship changes the atmosphere. Let's change the atmosphere of our lives today!

Testimony

I had very little knowledge or experience in "soaking" when I began coming to Kathy's on Tuesday mornings. She and her staff taught me about stopping my "analyzing" of what was going on and just resting in the presence of Jesus, receiving from Him all that He wants to give me, and truly enjoying Him. Kathy also encouraged me to soak in His presence every day, which I've been doing. After I get up in the morning, I have some Scripture and devotional time, and then I turn on my Ipod. I compiled a "soaking" category on it with worshipful instrumental music. Then I close my eyes and invite Jesus to come. AND HE DOES! Sometimes I am aware of what He's pouring into me and sometimes I'm not. It doesn't matter—when I am done, He's restored my soul and prepared me for whatever the day will bring me. I'm noticing such a difference in me and even how my day goes! I sense His presence, peace, power, voice, freedom, love and acceptance in ways I never have before. This comes with a warning, though—He is VERY habit-forming :-) I'm so grateful to God for Kathy's ministry to me in this way, using the gifts God has given her and her staff to encourage and teach me in experiencing intimacy with my Lord.

Julie S.

CHAPTER 10

Soaking and Resting in Him

Soaking and resting in the Lord is an important part of growing intimate in your walk with Jesus. Intimacy with Jesus, what is that, you may be asking? It is getting to know Jesus, His heart and spending alone time with Him. Jesus desires a personal relationship with us. He wants to spend time with us and fellowship with us; one of the ways He does this is through us entering into a quiet time with Him. Soaking is putting on some soft Christian music and simply lying or sitting in the Lord's presence. In this chapter I will walk you through the different ways we soak, why we soak and what you need to soak.

In this day and age we live in a fast paced society. We are always on the run going in all different directions. We are busy offering people our suggestions, thoughts and ideas and some of you just like to talk, talk, talk! My best friend talks all time; whether it is to the Lord, to me, her family and even herself. She loves to talk! Now I do want to say she is also an amazing listener. She isn't one of those annoying people who talk too much; she justs like to gab or hear herself I think! Who knows! Anyway, even if we aren't a talker, God still needs us to slow down and just be still and listen to Him. If we are busy talking all the time; how can we possibly hear God? God desires to communicate with us, refresh us, refill us and have us just sit at His feet. One of the ways we can do this is through soaking.

In order to start soaking with the Lord, you will need to find your quiet place and a place that is free of distractions. I suggest your living room, bedroom or prayer room. Put on some soft worshipful music and find a comfortable position and listen to the music. As you are starting to soak, you need to learn how to disconnect your mind and the thoughts that are running through it from the day. It will take an average of 15-20 minutes to disengage your brain when you first start, so don't get discouraged; it is normal. What are some practical tips for trying to disengage from the world and connect with the Father? Here are some tips:

- Blank out your thoughts.
- Speak in English; praise you Jesus, thank you Lord. Be careful not to pray and give Him your prayer list or your mind will start going.
- Pray in the Spirit (tongues).
- Listen to instrumental music.
- Reflect on a vision you had with Jesus.
- Put yourself in your "happy place," such as the beach or sitting by the fire.

Continue by trying to enter into His presence. Tell Him "Lord I am here for You, whatever You want." Then be quiet and just listen. Focus on the music if you start to get distracted and your mind starts to wonder. Really press into the drums or piano, or focus on the words, and see if the Lord will speak to you through the words the musicians are singing. If you are not "feeling" the music, then change the music.

There are different types of music people soak to:

- Worship music—Soft worshipful music usually from well known artists and songs you are familiar with. A very popular way to start soaking is by listening to worship music, and singing along can help you stay focused and enter into the Lord's presence. After a while, you may find you need to lean away from worship music during your soaking time because you know the songs and are familiar with them. This can make it a challenge to soak, because you are getting into the music and not trying to focus on resting in the Lord.
- Instrumental music—Music without words such as piano or violin which can be very anointed. The water and nature music you can obtain might also be a type you would enjoy. People like instrumental music because they find it calming and relaxing. For people who have a lot on their mind this can be good, because they can get caught up in the waves and nature sound and try to relax. It can also be a challenge because since there are no words, their minds might keep going because they don't have anything to focus on. Find what soothes you and what works for you.
- Prophetic music—This music will go up and down, will be free flowing and not always songs you know. It can be songs played over and over, or songs that really talk about the presence of the Lord and being with Him. There are many great prophetic worship artists who know how to usher in the manifest presence of the Lord. I believe this is the goal in soaking we should try to obtain. The wonderful thing about prophetic music is that it is always changing. You need to be conscious

that you don't get caught up in singing while the music is playing otherwise you will find yourself worshiping instead of soaking.

I suggest you frequently change your soaking music. As I look back over the years I can see that my music taste changes about every 4-6 months. You don't want to get bored with your music. If the music has stopped bringing you into the presence you have probably grown through that music. There is nothing wrong with the music, you have been moved to a deeper intimacy with the Lord and need something that can minister to you where you are at.

You need to also find musicians whose voices you like. Do you prefer a man or a woman? Do you have a favorite artist? Stock up on good music! Borrow some music from a friend to find out what you like and then go out and purchase it! Don't copy it or download it to your Ipod, buy it yourself! Music that has been copied isn't going to be anointed! We as Christians should not be copying music for others to use freely. We need to give the musicians and their companies the proper respect and money they deserve for their work. If we copy music it is stealing and against the Word of God! Be honest, respectful and pay what is due the musicians!

When you have the music you like to listen to make yourself a few different play lists on your Ipod. This can help not take you out of the spirit. Once in a while a soaking album will have a more upbeat prophetic song in the line up. This can take us out of the presence of God and leave us irritated. Therefore, delete that song from your Ipod or create a list that helps usher you into the presence of God. I also prefer, when I am soaking on the floor, to have my Ipod, Ipod dock or stereo near me, so I can change songs without getting up and out of the presence. I often wear my ear buds connected to my Ipod, so everything is right there and I can blast myself with music without interrupting other people in my home. If you are not being moved by the Spirit, change your music. Don't sit there stumped and not able to enter in! By having all these devices within your reach you can easily do this.

How you set up your room and what you need is up to you. Here are some things we have done. Please feel free to adapt any to your personal needs.

Room Set-Up:
- Make a prayer room or "secret place" in your home where you can be alone with the Lord. An area in your home where peace can abide, that isn't in a high traffic area and in which the children do not usually play.
- Turn your bedroom into a sanctuary. We did a replica of the tabernacle in our bedroom with royal-like materials and materials to represent the veil.
- Soak in the bathtub. The bath is a great place to soak and worship the Lord. Your distractions are minimized, light some candles and put in your music.

Optional items to have in your room:
- Candles-scented can be relaxing and help you enter in and they also create a nice atmosphere if soaking while it is still dark out.
- Water Fountain—Can be very soothing.
- Prayer Quilt—We had one made with our ministry logo, the cross, healing scriptures, a dove, hearts and hands.

Every part of the quilt represented something special including, white and leaf material on back for healing and water around the edge for the living water.

- Anointed materials—they used them in Old Testament times and we use them now. Go to the store and ask the Holy Spirit for discernment and start laying your hands on some material. Purchase a piece 2-3 yards take it home and anoint it, worship with it, lie on it or under it and pray with it.

What to bring with you:
- Bring your water, coffee or tea to the floor with you.
- Put a notepad and pen next to you for revelation.

Preventing distractions:
- Lock up pets; they seem to be sensitive to the spirits.
- Turn off your phones, put them on silence or vibrate.
- Put a blanket on the floor to prevent against cold, smelly or dirty floors. Use a blanket to keep warm. Stay out of drafts; cold is a distraction.

Getting started:
- Start with high praise, move to worship and end up in soaking. My friend and I always say good worship is high praise on our feet, move to worship on your knees and end up soaking on your face. If preferred, you can start out with slow music soaking.
- Go when the Lord calls and don't delay. Often we miss His presence because we are busy doing for Him instead of being with Him. When you feel Him calling; go at once.
- Anoint yourself and take communion.

- Pray in the spirit (tongues) if you get distracted until you can bring your mind back into focus.
- Suggestions of soaking music to listen too. I enjoy the following musicians for soaking music:

  —Amy Thompson
  —Laura Rhinehart
  —Terry MacAlmon
  —Jason Upton
  —Dennis Jernigan
  —Laura Woodley
  —Ric Pino
  —Watchmen for the Nations
  —Alberto and Kimberly Rivera
  —Daniel Brymer
  —Rita Springer
  —Misty Edwards
  —Tina Bolinger

Benefits of soaking:

- Impartation—During soaking God will drop words of knowledge, direction and discernment into our spirit. I also believe He imparts wisdom and scripture for a particular situation for us in the future or someone we are going to minister to. Did you ever think, where did that come from? I believe in these moments of soaking with God that He does some deep impartations that we use at a later time.
- Resting—Often as we soak we will not even know what we receive. You might feel like you are almost in a state of a deep sleep; yet you are conscious. I believe we receive much during these times and sometimes God

simply does it because we need to rest, be refreshed and refilled.

- An act of worship—By stilling ourselves to rest in His presence, we are telling God that He is important enough for us to stop what we are doing and just be with Him. We are giving Him first place and worshiping Him by doing this.

There is no right or wrong way to soak. You can use any of the above suggestions as the Holy Spirit leads. The only thing you need to do is come with a receiving heart, put in some music and sit back or lie down and relax and receive or rest in the Lord. In the times where we feel we aren't hearing from the Lord it is in those times we need to do it the most. Soaking is wonderful and during soaking you will discover and encounter a level of intimacy with the Lord that you have never known. I bless you as you start this endeavor!

About the Author

Kathy DeGraw is the founder and president of DeGraw Ministries. She strengthens, teaches, trains and equips believers to experience the fullness of God through hosting conferences, teaching schools and other events. She has a clear and unique gift of discernment and operates in a strong healing and deliverance anointing. She believes in calling forth the glory of the Lord to heal, set free and deliver.

She stretches believers to reach for more so they can be equipped for the ministry God is calling them to. She believes the more ministries that are established, more people can be set free from the bondages of the enemy. She believes in breaking down religious and denominational barriers, and in her weekly meetings equips believers in denominational churches to live a spirit filled life and transform their churches.

She is passionate about worship and intimacy with the Lord and believes the Lord is rising up a new generation of worshipers who will worship him in freedom, spirit and truth. She believes spending time with the Lord on the floor prostrate seeking His face is the key to intimacy and relationship with Him.

Kathy is the author of *Time to Set the Captives Free* a book on starting your own deliverance ministry. She has also written *The Sky's the Limit*. This book instructs you how to create an amazing Kids Club outreach program to reach out to the children in your community and grow your church. She has received the American Author's Association, 2009 Golden Quill Award for this book.

Kathy and her husband, Ron, have three teenage children, Dillon, Amber, and Lauren and make their home in Grandville, Michigan.

For further information, or to be in touch with Kathy, contact:

DeGraw Ministries
P.O. Box 65
Grandville, Michigan 49468
Website: www.degrawministries.org
Email: Kathy@degrawministries.org

OTHER BOOKS BY KATHY DEGRAW:

Sky's the Limit by CSS Publishing

Time to Set the Captives Free by West Bow Printing

Would you like to see your manuscript become a book?

If you are interested in becoming a PublishAmerica author, please submit your manuscript for possible publication to us at:

acquisitions@publishamerica.com

You may also mail in your manuscript to:

**PublishAmerica
PO Box 151
Frederick, MD 21705**

www.publishamerica.com

Breinigsville, PA USA
23 February 2011
256169BV00009B/2/P